Heart Healing

13 Principles of Emotional Self Healing

Lysa Black

Heart Healing: 13 Principles of Emotional Self Healing
By Lysa Black

Published by
Transcendent Publishing
P.O. Box 66202
St. Pete Beach, FL 33736
www.transcendentpublishing.com

Transcendent
——Publishing——

ISBN-10: 0-9987576-7-5
ISBN-13: 978-0-9987576-7-4

Printed in the United States of America.

Dedication

I dedicate this book to you, beautiful soul. I honour you for what you have survived, what you have had to endure.

I trust that you can safely navigate the terrain where you find yourself right now. You have overcome so much; I know that your challenges today will only prove to develop you further. I know you can rise up to your current situation; it's time to sink into your soul, it will be your way through.

By healing my wounds, my eyes have been opened to the perfection inherent in us all.

I see your light, I believe in you.

~Lysa Black

Acknowledgements

From my soul - Thank you so much to my Mum, Ann Hill & my Dad, Greg Hill who showed up so perfectly in order to teach me what I needed to step into my power. I honour you for the lives you have lived and hold you both dear to my heart.

My dear Husband Abinadi, your love for me was my first healing miracle from above. Your love has supported me in every way to step deeper into my truth and honour the soul that I am. My light shines now because it was first witnessed by you; I opened to see my own light through the power and intensity of your own.

My dear friend, Gina Brown you are amazing. Your gifts of acceptance, honesty and love have inspired me to shift more fully into my truth. Through our friendship, I continually find myself and fall more in love with who I am because of the enormity of my love for you. I could never have made my way here without your wisdom, guidance and gifts.

Thank you to all of my clients who have believed in me, and followed me on the path to self healing. Your courage, determination and faith constantly inspire me. I wrote this book for each of you.

Contents

Foreword

Congratulations for picking up this book!

You are about to go on a journey with the amazing Lysa Black. This journey will take you to the very depths of your own heart, where deep healing can take place.

Lysa will gently and expertly guide you to discover what it is that your heart and soul is crying out for. Over the past two decades I have explored many different healers and workshops but it was finding Lysa that was the real turning point for true heart healing for me. Lysa's ability to guide you to true profound change is rare in my experience.

I have worked with Lysa as both a coaching client and as part of her Heart Healing Circle so I can tell you that this process will have an impact. You will see change.

I am excited for you as you begin your healing journey with Lysa and I wish you blessings and joy on your journey. You are safe in Lysa's hands.

~Paula McFarlane

Introduction

The Golden Buddha

Over three hundred years ago, the Burmese army were planning an attack to invade Thailand (formerly Siam). The Siamese monks were in possession of an amazing Buddha statue. This statue is over 10 feet tall and weighs more than 2.5 tonnes. It is made of solid gold and is valued today at $200 million dollars.

The monks were determined to protect the shrine that meant so much to them. While it was sacred and priceless to them; they knew that the Burmese army would stop at nothing to steal and destroy the statue because of its tremendous monetary value. They covered the Golden Buddha with 12 inches of clay knowing that the army would totally ignore it and think it to be worthless. Sadly, the monks were slaughtered in the invasion, and the secret of the Golden Buddha stayed hidden for two centuries. The Buddha itself though, remained safe.

In the mid 1950's, the monastery next to the Buddha statue was to be relocated to make room for a new highway. The monks arranged for a crane to come and move the 'clay' Buddha to its new location. When the crane started to lift the statue, it was much heavier than expected and began to crack. Wanting to protect the priceless shrine, the monks lowered it back down and decided to wait until the next day to bring in more powerful equipment. In the dark of night, the head monk took his flashlight and went out to make sure the Buddha was adequately covered. When the light of the flashlight shone into the crack of the clay, he saw a glimmer, a reflection of something underneath the clay. He immediately started to carefully chisel away shards of clay to find that the glimmer grew brighter. Hours later, and all of the clay removed, he was in the presence of a Buddha made of solid gold. The Temple of the Golden Buddha now resides in Bangkok, Thailand. Every year, millions of people go there to see this magnificent work of art and to worship at his feet. And to think, it may never have been uncovered.

In order to investigate the shimmer that Monk found under the clay, he needed to destroy what was known to him to be a sacred relic.

We are our own sacred relic's, but in this modern world of trying to fit in with others, we run the rat race of a busy life, conform to social pressures and change ourselves in an attempt to please others by being a better wife, lover, mother, employee, daughter or friend. It becomes very easy for us to forget our purity, light and divinity and cover ourselves in clay in an attempt to protect ourselves. Through this process, we forget who we really are - our purpose, our power and lose the peace we deserve.

When we were born we knew who we were and enjoyed the connection with our power and light. As we observed those around us behaving and talking as though they had forgotten their truth, for fear of rejection and isolation we began playing the same game. As a means of self-protection, we allowed others and ourselves to put clay on us until we were covered, so we could not shine and live our true purpose. We effectively buried our true nature and rejected ourselves. We gave away our power and forgot our own light. We let our 'ego' keep us safe and plunged ourselves further into experiences of misery, suffering, doubt, fear and loneliness.

If you are reading this, you are starting to see the cracks through your clay. You are feeling curious about yourself and will feel nervous or excited about this sacred opportunity to venture into yourself. To shed the clay and reclaim the truth of who you are; to reclaim your purpose, power and peace. Put simply, Heart Healing will provide you with the opportunity to remove any false unfitting ideas of who you think you are and reclaim something precious and profound; the truth of who you really are.

I am here as your guide, to invite you to look within and encourage you to feel curious excitement about pulling back some of the clay of who you have thought yourself to be and find your gold within.

I believe that before coming into this experience of life, we all held the truth of ourselves as pure, divine, loving, expansive beings capable of experiencing any desire, and manifesting any wish.

It is with great joy that I invite you on a journey with me as your guide. I offer caution, this work will deeply challenge you to acknowledge the ego story that has been your clay covering. The resistance from your ego will show itself in varying degrees of strength. I will teach you how to harness that resistance so that it may directly guide you to bring healing to the lies you have unknowingly held about yourself. Pay close attention to your feelings; the wash of tingles, light and strength is the tide of truth returning.

Care of: http://close2bliss.wordpress.com/2011/03/30/the-story-of-the-golden-buddha/

LYSA BLACK

What is Heart Healing?

"*Eventually you will come to understand that love heals everything, and love is all there is.*"

Gary Zukav

LYSA BLACK

Heart Healing is a process of reclaiming the truth of who we are. Our heart pain invites us to look within, to find the heart wounds that we have unknowingly held as false assumptions about who we are.

It's the recurring patterns of emotional pain in our life that first invites us onto the path of self healing. Emotional pain is actually an invitation to pay attention; a request for us to look within ourselves so that we may uncover what needs to be healed. Heart ache and heart pain actually signify heart wounds. Heart wounds are the misperceptions we have inherited about who we are; the ideas we hold about our identity that are out of alignment with our soul truth.

Pain is a request from our soul to listen and be aware of what we telling ourselves about 'who' we think we are. We have all forgotten the truth of who we are, giving our power away to those closest to us when we're young in an attempt to find acceptance, validation and love.

As little children, we didn't understand or appreciate the wounds within our parents, siblings and social world. We presumed everyone was whole, healthy, and functioning from love. So, when we experienced non-love as a consequence of fear based wounded behaviour, it confused us. We chose to withhold judgement and condemnation from those near and dear to us, and instead chose to make ourselves, wrong, bad, and incomplete. This process of applying clay to ourselves and permitting others to cover us in clay served to protect us for a time. It allowed the world to make sense. Otherwise irrational and unloving behaviours could be justified and explained because it was 'I' who was the problem.

It is our current emotional experiences today which will directly lead us back to the memories that require our attention and revision. Some of the confusing and complicated experiences of our past were situations where we made conclusions about who we are, what we're capable of and the meaning of life, love and everything else. No matter how loving or unloving our upbringing was, the complex, confusing and difficult experiences we have all endured prompted us to make certain conclusions about why things were the way they were. Rather than blame anyone else, inquire or continually feel confused; we all made little conclusions about who we are to give ourselves a sense of certainty and assurance. We all yearn for a sense of continuity and stability that nothing outside of us is wrong; we chose instead to conclude that our challenges must stem from the truth that we are simply unlovable, unworthy or undeserving.

When we are holding onto concepts of ourselves that are untrue, our spirit sends us a painful sensation. In order to communicate that what we believe about ourselves is false, our soul sends us emotional pain. Heart pain indicates that we are holding onto a lie about who we are. However, when we are inexperienced in this process we come to believe that every painful emotional response in our life is actually proof that what we do believe about ourselves is in fact true. The ego story that we all form about who we are, what love is and what life is all about becomes the unconscious script that we play out over and over; making our heart wounds self-fulfilling prophecies. Yes, the false ideas we formed of ourselves long ago, actually cause us to unconsciously re-create those past painful experiences today. Not to make us suffer or as punishment, but as a loving invitation from our own soul to pay attention, look within and heal the misperception of who we think we are.

Heart pain has a way of grabbing our attention. While it can be easy to get lost in a vain attempt to numb, suppress or escape our pain, inevitably it will return over and over until we find the courage to stop what we are doing and start looking at our feelings, our lives, our patterns, and our wounds.

The pain is only intended to get our attention long enough to invite us to seek the clarity and confirmation of the truth of who we really are; our true identity. Until we heal our heart wounds, we will unconsciously seek out those same familiar patterns. When the pain gets too intense, we all choose to open up and shift into looking within. Healing is a process of using your pain to return to the memories of moments when you unknowingly accepted a false idea about who you are. As we uncover the lies that originally forged our heart wounds, you can then call on your higher power to remind you of the truth of who you really are. Receiving the truth from your higher power, will allow you to remember your truth, to support you to realign with your soul and feel an emotional shift that is unmistakeable.

The value of heart healing is profound; once our heart wounds have been healed, we free ourselves from our old patterns and instead start creating and forming what our hearts and souls truly long for. Manifesting our heart's desires is our personal reward confirming the healing which has taken place in our hearts. Receiving the love, connection, and fulfilment we all yearn for is a rich delight, but recognising that we have healed our own pattern is truly empowering. Healing one single wound and its accompanying pattern is often all we need to invest ourselves more intently on continuing our heart healing to open ourselves up to receive everything we truly desire.

I will lead you into the heart healing paradigm, where emotional pain is a gift. This pain will guide you straight to wounds where your misperceptions were formed. Your sensitive awareness to your feelings will now become your asset. I will teach you how to understand the messages your emotions bring so that you can use your feelings to find wounds, receive the truth and be healed.

It's our unhealed wounds from the past that end up driving many of our choices and behaviours today; keeping us stuck in repeating patterns. These patterns are not intended as punishment, but rather they are a loving invitation for you to see that what you believe about yourself, is untrue. We can only know what is untrue by how it feels; truth feels: loving, enlightening, expansive and joyful. Lies feel: scary, weakening, confusing, overwhelming and depressive.

We come to the earth as babes in total connection with our truth, our light and our lovability. It is intended that we will all forget the truth of our true nature and instead become covered in clay concluding that we are: 'undeserving', 'unworthy' and 'unlovable'. We are here to experience contrast; we knew the power of our truth, but we didn't know what happens when we forget that truth. The act of forgetting our true nature and becoming disconnected and detached gives us passage into the world of duality. Duality, allows us to experience the polar opposites of everything we knew in the previous world; a place where we can feel fear, scarcity, aggression, oppression and powerlessness. These composite 'negative' emotions carry value and depth because they actually allow us to experience and comprehend the true value of their composite companions: love, connection, joy and authentic power.

The very process of forgetting our identity and experiencing the world of duality allows us to discover the tremendous value and gift it is to be who we are.

This is a rich and exciting journey; you never know where it may lead. You can expect your journey to self healing to be incredibly eye-opening and curious, you will find treasures and new richness at every step and come to respect and appreciate yourself far more than ever before. My role is to guide you through the principles to heart healing so that you can start using your patterns to usher in the clarity of your truth. The truth of who you are is the healing power of this work; it will come to you in images, thoughts, and feelings. Any feelings of peace, calm, comfort, joy or love will confirm that you have reclaimed your truth, and you will see your recurring patterns fall away to confirm the healing that has taken place.

Tools for Healing

I would like to suggest two powerful tools for you to utilise to support yourself in this self healing process. The first is 'Breathing Through' and the second is 'Creating a Sanctuary'.

Breathing Through

Firstly we will prepare ourselves to breathe through what unfolds. When we can see ourselves in a recurring pattern, it is normal and natural to go into mental overload trying to figure out what is happening, plan a way to get out of it, or analyse the situation in the hope that you can intellectually fix it. Naturally our minds can become frazzled with too much information or our hearts feel overloaded with too much unprocessed emotion; we can feel like we're spinning out of control (not the fun merry-go-round type of spin!).

It is for this reason that I encourage you to lean on the power of your breath in these moments. Heart healing is something that doesn't need to be rushed. Being calm and centred is the fastest way to use the tools I will share so you can take the steps to get the insight to heal and shift out of the patterns you can see.

Normally our breathing is unconscious, although it is with our awareness and attention that we can guide our own breath deeper and fuller. This gives us the awareness to centre our consciousness back towards our heart and reach a calm, gentle place where we can be receptive to guidance and healing.

Being able to use the power and focus of your breath to be

with any feelings that come up, will provide a supportive space for you to make progress on your self healing journey. Your breath is a powerful tool to stay in the moment and actively/consciously calm yourself.

If you start to feel frazzled, overloaded or out of control in an emotional situation, instantly say to yourself, "breathe in". Use this verbal cue, to focus on breathing in deeply and calmly, and then remind yourself to "Breathe out", allowing your tension to increasingly depart as all of your breath leaves your lungs.

If it helps, count to 10 with each inhale and exhale. After doing this a few times you will find your heart rate slows, your breathing deepens and you'll feel yourself enter a new space, one that is calm, centred and powerful.

Every time you pick up this book, I suggest you begin to practice placing a few moments of awareness on your breath. You'll be amazed at the instant shift this exercise will have on bringing you calmness and clarity in any situation, preparing you perfectly for heart healing.

Creating a Sanctuary

The second tool I would like to share with you is called 'Creating a Sanctuary'. Creating a visualised place or sanctuary where you can feel safe and secure is vital as you prepare to go within and allow healing to take place. When we are unsure and fearful we can become stuck; resistance occurs as we try to hold on. It's this unconscious holding on, that prevents the necessary flow of change into our emotional world. Carl Jung taught, "What we resist persists".

As we create a sanctuary perfectly designed with our tastes in mind, we are empowered to generate supportive feelings such as: love, safety, and assurance. With the support of these powerful positive emotions we begin to open up and prepare ourselves for a powerful healing experience.

It is powerful and supportive to create an emotionally soothing sanctuary to aid yourself in your self healing journey. Your sanctuary is a visualised, location created from your memory or imagination; a place where you can feel calm, safe and secure.

Your sanctuary can be anywhere or anything you choose. From the quiet of the bush, to the calm of the seashore, the thick lays of green surrounding you in a jungle or you may yearn for the expansive vista from a tall solitary building. You can choose a place that you have been to, or create an entirely new place that you have never seen with your own eyes. You are completely free to design and create an environment that is most supportive for you to feel loved, safe and cared for. As you access your inner architect you will construct and arrange your sanctuary as you feel intuitively led. It will take time to form your sanctuary according to your heart's desires; it may even be a work in progress for some time. Every time you visit your sanctuary, you are free to adjust the surroundings to your preference and sharpen details in every area. This will become your place of refuge.

According to your own preference and desire imagine a special place where you can go in your mind anytime where you can feel grounded, loved and secure. When you feel complete in your design, allow yourself to mentally, emotionally and spiritually come to this sacred place as often as you desire. The more time you spend here, the more you can deepen into feeling relaxed, cared for and serene. I suggest you create your sanctuary in preparation to starting your heart healing journey, and likewise, frequent this special space as often as you like.

Preparation

LYSA BLACK

1. **Heart healing evokes the presence of three separate parts of yourself:**

   Your inner child. This is our true authentic nature. Who we are as young children, between three and seven years is the closest representation of who we really are: our authentic identity. That was the time when we had implicit trust in ourselves, we lived in our power accepting and appreciating ourselves.

   Your ego. This is the part of you that was born in suffering. The role of your ego is to protect you from harm and pain; it's like a stern loving parent. If you step out of line and head towards something 'dangerous' it will scream, call out or berate you for your reckless behaviour. What your ego says is not completely true, its perspective is completely limited to your past experiences and what it concluded from those past experiences. The role of the ego is to keep us within the boundaries of what we've known and think is safe, stepping outside of what we know signals danger to the ego. Ego resists change, new experiences, and stepping towards anything that it thinks has caused you pain.

   Your spirit: (Your soul, essence, light or higher self). This is the part of you that lived before you were born, and will live on even after your earthly body dies. Your spirit always knows and remembers the truth of who you are. It will communicate to you through your feelings. Pain signals that we believe something about ourselves which is untrue. Our spirit is always asking and inviting us to remember our full truth and step back into our power and light. When we live from our soul, we are naturally calm, loving, generous and guided. Living from your soul allows you to create and manifest the sincere desires of your heart. Unlike your ego, your soul invites and beckons you to try new experiences, opening you up more than you've known, helping you to expand and open to all that is. Your soul intends to experience the widest variety of richness in life; the soul loves to learn and grow from everything you create in your world. For your soul, there are no bad experiences, just opportunities to remember, readjust and recreate. Every experience provides clarity on what it is that you truly desire, and how you can easily manifest it into your world.

2. Resistance signals that we are on the right track.

As we deepen into the soul part of our being, our ego feels afraid and apprehensive. It will send us feelings of fear, concern, apprehension and worry to try and prevent us from shifting into closer alignment with our truth. Ego fears that it will not be needed or valued if we live from our soul. Ego is convinced that the world is a scary, unsure, unpredictable place that could hurt or harm you. As you follow your heart, your inner guidance or attempt to live from your soul, ego will react; send strong feelings requesting that you abandon the plan. We will be learning to use this resistance as a sign that you are on the right track. Ego will only cause a strong emotional reaction within us if we are headed towards the truth of our soul. In time, you will come to use this resistance to confirm that the choice before you is actually leading you to more freedom, love and expansion.

Prepare yourself to experience sensations, all kinds of different feelings, movement and emotion within your body. You are safe to experience any sensation that surfaces. I will act as your guide, supporting you on this rich exciting adventure helping you to use your feelings to navigate your own path to heart healing.

Chapter 1 – Pain Calls for Healing

"Some people are afraid of what
they might find...

but you have to crawl into your wounds to
discover where your fears are.

Once the bleeding starts
the cleansing can begin"

Tori Amos

Pain is something that we all experience. From our first breath to our last, pain visits us all. I used to despise pain, I would go to great lengths to avoid it, escape it or attempt to numb it. In the story I share below, my pain had reached a whole new level of intensity. I now honour this pain because it actually became my doorway to peace.

I thought my compulsive overeating was my biggest problem. The longer I felt trapped and overwhelmed in this problem, the clearer I saw it was a mirage. My compulsive binge eating was merely the symptom, it was my fear of anxiety that was causing me to go rushing to the fridge. It was my big dirty secret.

My compulsive binge eating was merely the symptom.

I weighed 99kg at the age of seventeen and had just conquered a five year journey to shed 30kg, I was supposed to feel successful, instead I had to face the truth that my excess weight was not the source of all of my problems as I had naively assumed. And now that my excuse had been removed, I truly had nowhere to hide. I had just had a huge fall-out with my Mum. My latest boyfriend (who I didn't even really like) had just broken up with me, and it had devastated my world. I was working as a weight loss counsellor in Australia, and all of a sudden I felt like I was the one in need of counselling.

Instead I had to face the truth that my excess weight was not the source of all of my problems; as I had naively assumed.

I would sneak off to a cafe down the road and buy an ice cream for lunch (I had not eaten chocolate, ice cream or cake for over a year!), then knowing one just wasn't enough, I would travel another few blocks down the road to buy another. I felt too ashamed to have the store owner see me buy two!

I knew I was out of control. I was hurting in a way that I couldn't comprehend. Being thin had been my dream for so long, but it was not what I had expected. I had told myself that if I was thin, then I could find love. It was my search for true love and connection that had motivated this epic transformation, but now that I had arrived, I could see that men found me more attractive, but they didn't love me. I was frightened; I had told myself that my weight was my only problem for so long that I had come to believe it. Now, I was here: thin and I still felt unlovable. My whole world felt like it was falling apart. I was afraid that anyone would find out how crazy I was. I knew I needed to hide my binge eating because I knew I was in trouble; the worst kind of trouble... I didn't know what was wrong with me!

I made the call to quit my job. I wasn't able to have any real conversations with my client's, because it would trigger my own internal pain. I would become a blubbering mess, not professional or even sane, to say the least. I had seen a psychotherapist at a local university seeking admission to their new 'Mindfulness' program to help with my compulsive bingeing and diet obsession. But I pulled the short straw and didn't make it in, I was devastated.

I remember wandering down the main street of Woolongabba, in Brisbane, Australia and seeing a sign that I had never noticed before advertising, 'Gestalt Therapy' counselling. I went straight up and made an appointment. During the session, the counsellor tried to help me express the pain I could feel inside, but nothing would pass my lips. I couldn't even raise a peep to express the depth of pain that consumed me within. The dam wall inside me had broken open but I was incapable of sharing the rushing mix of emotions that filled me. I was in total and utter confusion, all I knew was that being dissatisfied with life, was something that you shouldn't talk about. How I was 'feeling' had never been allowed out before, and I didn't know where to begin.

I knew I needed to get out of town, get away and process my internal crumbling in a place where no one knew me, where I could be alone in my pain and explore it like new terrain. I held a huge garage sale, sold everything except my favourite eight dresses and bought a one way ticket to Cairns. As I flew out of Brisbane, I left behind a long list of rules:

1. You have to care about everybody.

2. You can't be late, stingy or dirty.

3. Always smile at strangers.

4. Be the good girl.

5. Family comes first.

6. Always be responsible and reliable.

7. Don't talk back.

8. Don't talk to strangers.

9. Never express your true feelings.

10. Spend all of your time, energy and money making everyone else happy.

I was off and it was damn well liberating! The searing emotional pain I felt within had created a monumental shift in how I lived my life! Now was the time for rule breaking, now was the time for exploration, and now was the time to not give a damn about what anybody else thought.

Pain is such a powerful tool, because it is so effective at getting our attention. Our pain resists and defies elimination because it has a message that it must deliver. I believe that pain is a call for healing. Pain is a request from our soul to heal. Pain is the result of a lie, a wound in our heart. The pain resides smack bang in the place where we believe something that is contrary to our truth. The lie was formed long ago, and pain is the signal from our soul that the time has come to allow healing.

So no matter how long, hard or elaborately we attempt to manage this pain; hide from it, numb it or outwit it; it will continue to visit us to remind us that we are not who we think we are.

Heart Healing Magic

1) Write down the one feeling that you have been resisting the most recently. Go ahead and name that one feeling.

2) Lie down with your eyes closed; lie softly, palms facing upward with your whole body limp and supple. Feel the sensations throughout your body, searching for any sensations that feel painful. Hold the intention of witnessing your pain. Allow yourself to travel from head to toe in search of tightness, stiffness, numbness, aching, searing heat or swirling sensations. Your aim is to be with the feelings you encounter to lovingly acknowledge their presence.

3) Give yourself the freedom to have an honest conversation with your soul:

E.g. "I'm really hurting here, can you help me? Can you protect me and guide me as I search for my pain, so that I can welcome healing in to my life?"

Healing Affirmations

- I now allow myself to see.

- I courageously look within.

- I listen to my pain.

- My pain shows me my lies.

- Pain is my doorway to healing.

Chapter 2 –
Seeing the Pattern

"*Nothing ever goes away*

until it teaches us what we need to know."

Pema Chodron

Our patterns of pain invite us to healing. The pain is only intended to get our attention so that we can become aware of the ideas we're holding onto that are hurting us. When we believe an idea that is not in alignment with our truth, it will generate emotional pain so that we can know it is untrue. This process gets our attention so that we can find the lie at the centre of our heart wound.

My first boyfriend, Mr. Yamaguichi was Japanese, originally my 'language partner' at university. Our friendship moved on from vocabulary to romance over the space of nine months. He was such a great guy, he had an open mind, a fun outgoing personality, he listened and I knew he really cared about me. After eight months together, he suddenly found out that he had a hole in the lens of his eye; specialist surgery could correct the problem, but without immediate attention his sight could deteriorate irreparably. He needed to return to Japan quickly to have an operation. So, suddenly my first romance halted and I had only days to farewell my first love.

The sudden departure shook my world. I struggled through every day feeling disconnected by distance to the only love and care I had known. Later I would realise how familiar his absence was to me. It felt familiar because it was familiar, my parents had separated frequently over my life. At the time Mr. Yamaguchi left I was lost in despair, thinking forlornly about my departed love when really underneath it all, I was just feeling the pain of my parents frequent separating all over again. The painful difference this time was that I wasn't looking from the outside at my parents separating; I was experiencing it personally for myself.

Fast forward four months, Mr. Yamaguchi's operation was successful and he was furiously working two jobs to save enough money to come back to Australia for a longer period of time. It was like a heavy drug was wearing off me week by week, the longer we were apart the less I thought of him. I can now see that I fell in love with being loved. While we were discussing marriage just before he left, I now felt more and more reluctant to stay with him. I eventually expressed my desire to end our relationship. With one taste of 'love', I was hungry for more.

I can now see that I fell in love with being loved.

My next romantic leap was Mr. Caveman, an Australian who attended the same church as me. This man had been divorced, and I could tell he was still heart-broken. I was a sucker for a broken heart; my inner nurturer felt safe and comfortable attempting to console him in his pain. This had always been my role; it was where I felt safe and needed. But despite my love and care, there were times when Mr. Caveman would shut me out, he would retreat into the solitude and darkness of his cave if there was something difficult he didn't want to face. It reminded me so much of the pain I felt when mum and dad used to separate. When their arguments would escalate, they would both retreat into separate areas and I would be left alone.

I now have the hindsight to see how I specifically chose Mr. Caveman because deep down I knew that I could rely on him to play the role I was familiar with. I could rely on his caveman ways to keep me looping in the same pattern I knew. It's the familiar painful currents of our past that we can find ourselves swimming in as an adult. One part of us believes we deserve it: "This same experience happened to your parents, so it's going to happen to you too", our ego taunts. Another part of us is horrified that something that was so difficult and painful for us in the past, has now found its way into our own personal lives today. While I can now see that this pain was intended to bring me a valuable message, at this time in my life I was still deaf to the messenger and blind to my role in recreating the circumstances of my past.

Mr. Caveman and I broke up several times, both initiating the separation at different stages, but it was only a matter of time before we would become drawn back together again. It was an on-off saga that spanned three years of my life. Each time we would separate and then re-unite, the searing heartache felt so similar. I began to notice how familiar my heart pain felt each time we separated.

With heightened awareness, the pattern of pain linked to our separating became more obvious. Mr. Cave Man would repeatedly cut me off, recede into his cave and then days, weeks, months later come back with renewed commitment and stronger promises. I was a sucker for punishment! Finally after having one year apart, he moved back to Brisbane where I was living, invited me out to lunch the first chance he got, and spoke openly about his intention to marry me. I couldn't believe what I was hearing, my heart was swept away and all of the pain of our dysfunctional on-off relationship disappeared into the background as I gave myself over for the chance of what I hoped could be true love.

This time however, something was different, I could see clearer. Our heart pain has a way of developing our awareness. I began to recognise how he would shut me out when things got hard, just like my mum and dad did to one another when I was young. He would come and go repeatedly, recreating the separation saga my parents had shown me. I watched how his calm, composed, mature persona would melt under pressure to reveal a very angry and confused little boy. Finally, with more time and deeper conversations with Mr. Caveman, I finally allowed myself to clearly see the state of his heart. I saw that his heart was so broken, that it was incapable of loving me whether I was deserving of that love or not.

I ended the three year loop with Mr. Caveman; I was astonished by my choice, proud of my faith and ever hungry for true love. Mr. Caveman had clearly taught me that wounded hearts struggle to accept and offer love. While his promises and part-time offering of love were enough to satisfy me in the beginning, the longer we were together the less I found that experience of love acceptable; our heartache thus offers us clarity. As a child I knew separation, wounded hearts and a lack of love but it was intolerable for me now, the on-going pain I had endured over the last three years supported me to recognise and admit to myself that I required more. I required the love of someone who could accept me, someone who could stay with me and someone who could open up to me and really connect.

Our heart ache thus offers us clarity.

From then on my hunt hastened. I was all the more eager and curious about what love I would find out there. Did my Mr. Loving even exist? Could anyone ever actually truly love me as I am, for who I am? And who was I? I knew I had struggled to reveal who I really was in my dating attempts. I was fearful that if I showed anyone who I really was, then they would be able to criticise and attack me all the more. I was convinced there was something wrong with me, and the best line of defense seemed to be pretending I was someone that people could love. The challenging part was being fluid enough to accommodate a wide variety of varying preferences. I was just trying to be whoever I thought would be worthy of another's love, which inadvertently involved rejecting the truth of my real identity. I tried to only show the more appealing, desirable parts of myself: my kindness, my intellect, my generosity, my care. All of my effort was spent trying to hide my messiness, my selfishness, my judgements, my fears. It was incredibly taxing!

I was just trying to be whoever I thought would be worthy of another's love; which inadvertently involved rejecting the truth of my real identity.

My next series of first dates continued to confirm my fears. I didn't have to wait long to hear my date's attest: "You're too smart", "You're too opinionated", and "You're too loud!" Uh oh, even when I gave them my best, it wasn't good enough. My search for love intensified as I ran around dating rampantly in a pitiful bid to find acceptance. All the while I was secretly rejecting the truth of who I knew I was; oh the irony! The more furiously I tried to become lovable to the men I dated, the clearer my pattern of self-rejection became.

"Maybe I'm being too picky?" I wondered. I started to realise that I couldn't keep a front up my whole life. Who can pretend everyday of their lives that they are someone they are not? I got more honest with myself and acknowledged some of my less than desirable traits: "I'm self-righteous, I'm greedy, I'm arrogant", I declared to myself. "Why not, accept these parts of who I am and date someone who shares these qualities?" I mused. So, off I went to track down a new dating companion who could match my shadow side, maybe then I could stop hiding all of myself so much. That's when I fell for Mr. Suave. He was a flirt; he let all the girls know he found them attractive. He thought he knew everything, he definitely ticked the arrogant and self-righteous boxes. "Right let's try this on for size", I thought.

Dating Mr. Suave was a new experience, it felt easier. I didn't have to hide myself so much around him and I started to see some of the upsides of my qualities in him. He was arrogant, but he did share his opinion with authority. He was greedy, but he was also happy because he often got what he wanted. We seemed to come together effortlessly, we enjoyed one another's company. Mr. Suave definitely taught me the value and upside of parts of myself that I had judged and condemned as 'bad' my whole life. So, when he came to tell me '"It's over", my heart didn't hurt so much, I just felt despondent and confused. Mr. Suave touted some excuse about how I deserved a 'better' man but he was still leaving me like they all did. I reached a new conclusion; I have no idea what love is, nor how to find it!

So, my confidence in my own capacity to choose an ideal companion was flat tack zero at this stage and there was nothing else to do but seek out the most righteous, popular guy at church whom I didn't find attractive but who showed up on paper as the most reliable, organised, well-prepared man available; enter Mr. Safe.

This was a shot in the dark and it fell flat within weeks. Even thought I was in a 'committed' relationship with Mr. Safe, I couldn't bring myself to kiss him, and I couldn't control my flirtatious nature with other men. Mr. Suave and Mr. Safe just happened to be on the same soccer team. Mr. Suave had decided to ignore me while I was at his Saturday soccer game to cheer on my new boyfriend. Mr. Suave was refusing to acknowledge I was there, and I refused to be ignored. I drew nearer and nearer waiting for Mr. Suave to acknowledge me. In fact, I walked up to him so closely that I reached out and pushed his shoulder to assert, "I am here!" He still didn't verbally respond but instead chose to prod me back in the shoulder. Prod's turned shove's, the shove's turned to pushing and it wasn't long before we were in a full body wrestle down on the hard dusty ground in front of the whole soccer team.

Oh no! I felt like a hideous, thought-less vile creature once I'd realised what I'd done. Mr. Safe had been standing there with his team-mates watching the drama unfold the whole time. I tried to laugh off my blatant disrespect for Mr. Safe as I pulled myself up to standing. It was time to head home, with Mr. Safe sternly ignoring me from the driver's seat, we both sat in silence for the whole car ride home

Rather than condemn myself, my slip-up had revealed my heart; I was not emotionally committed to Mr. Safe and yet I didn't want it to end. He was brave, he wouldn't accept my blatant disrespect towards him and courageously walked to my home later that night to convey the news that 'we' were over! I fell into tears, profusely apologising and begging him to reconsider. It was truly pitiful! I knew I didn't want to be with him, and he had the guts to call me out on it. Yet the idea of being found 'unworthy of commitment' left my heart shattered and my mind frayed!

Why did I think choosing Mr. Safe would allow me to avoid my pattern of heartache? Why did I stay with him when I knew it wasn't right? And why was I a sobbing, delirious mess post break-up? I sat there hurting and confused, my heart was aching in the most overwhelming way, my soul was quivering in the corner and my ego loudly applauded the show and shouted, 'No one will ever want to be with you!' I sobbed and sobbed, and then from my utterly annihilated wasted state - I woke up!

I sat back and looked at the pain I could feel. It was searing, unending and intense! I knew it was not from Mr. Safe breaking up with me, there was more to this pain, and I got really curious... Something happened as soon as I got curious, time seemed to stand still; schedules, time, eating routines, everything fell away as I turned inwards in awe of something profound unfolding within me. My spiritual eyes seemed to be resisting the truth, they winced at the idea that my pattern of break-ups, could be emanating from within me.

When your past keeps replaying in the present, it's time to pay attention. Once I recognised that the problems consuming my life today were a reflection of the pain of my past, I began to wake up. I emerged into a whole new world, one where repeating pain was a powerful messenger that I was now intent on listening to.

***When your past keeps replaying in the present,
it's time to pay attention.***

During the painful experiences of my past, I had made my own conclusions:

1. I was unlovable.
2. Everyone leaves me.

3.   I don't deserve to be loved.

Telling myself these lies had allowed my parents fighting, separating and absence to make sense to me. But while they had allowed the confusion of my past to disappear, these ideas had become imbedded in my own soul and were now a prison controlling my whole life. The story I had adopted to help me make sense of my early years had become the script that I felt doomed to repeat over and over now as an adult.

I realised that my repeating pattern was a call to healing, it was my personal invitation to recall these past unconscious conclusions that I had made and re-evaluate them in the light of truth. If what we believe about ourselves causes us heart pain, then it is a lie. The experiences that we create in our lives are the clearest reflection of what we believe to be true. I found myself unfurling in a whole new magical world as I used every experience to help me develop my awareness of my heart wounds. I had manifested a mirror so big that the only thing I could now see was a deep reflection within myself. I knew that any uncomfortable experience that popped up in my life today had a history, and that history had a pattern of showing up continually in random occasions that were far enough apart and seeming so unrelated that they had escaped my conscious radar for some time. Nevertheless, it was the same old familiar pain that I felt in my heart that actually opened my eyes to finally see my patterns.

The clear vision to see our patterns can elude us for years, the characters and scenes of our heart pain can appear so new and different, that we can't recognise the correlation they have to our past. Nevertheless, it is the emotional currents of our lives which are always ebbing towards us, back from the beginning. When we made conclusions about ourselves that were untrue, they literally remained as unseen wounds, embedded in our soul. Any lies we unconsciously believed as children, become the script by which we choose, re-create and play out our old pain over and over again. Until the pain becomes so intense that it causes us to wake up and start looking within. I invite you to get curious the next time you feel pain. I invite you to look for the pattern underlying the recurring emotional pain in your life; this is how we know we are ready for heart healing.

Heart Healing Magic

1)   Write down the most recent painful experience that has come into your life. Write down the details of this painful experience in 50 words or less. Get clear on how and why it hurt you, and then ask yourself, how often has this pain visited me?

2)   Observe the frequency of this pain, it will allow you to identify your pattern. Use the familiar ache in your heart to bypass the details of the actual experience and instead use your feelings to bring your pattern into awareness.

3)   Write down which area of your life holds the most painful repeating pattern right now:

E.g:
- Weight/Body

- Career/Work

- Love/Relationship

- Social life/Friendship

- Money/Finances

Healing Affirmations

- My patterns have purpose.

- Recurring events help me to see.

- Repeating experiences lead me to wholeness.

- I now bravely see.

- Truth heals me.

LYSA BLACK

Chapter 3 –

Lies Form

Heart Wounds

LYSA BLACK

"Until you heal

the wounds from the past, you are

going to bleed."

Iyanla Vanzant

I know that lies create pain. Our souls are always aware of our truth, but many of the conclusions that we have drawn from our life experiences are misperceptions; lies going against our soul's truth. Our soul creates physical pain in the presence of a lie so that it may alert us to the destructive nature of this mistruth. Pain is not meant to hurt us beyond getting our attention; as soon as we listen and receive our truth, it ceases.

As the first born girl, I was incredibly confused by the constant arguing, fighting and mutual belittling that I observed between my parents. Being highly sensitive I could feel the unhealed wounds within them. I felt their pain as they unconsciously poked and pushed into each other's wounds. All three of us were in a great deal of pain; and I wanted to get out of it.

I didn't know how to get what I wanted and I didn't understand why my parents were fighting so intensely; I concluded that I was 'unlovable'. The day that I told myself, your parents fight because you are 'unlovable', allowed my whole world to suddenly make sense. The lies we hold in our heart wounds will seem ridiculous to any outside observer, our heart wounds only make sense to us. They are not logical, but emotionally they help make life feel understandable, comprehendible. The conclusion that I was unlovable brought me great relief because, if I was to blame for their arguments then, I could fix me and stop it all.

Without knowing it at the time, I had given myself the illusion of control. Because the pain of feeling so powerless was unbearable, I found solace in blaming myself. By placing the blame fairly on my own shoulders, I assumed the responsibility to find a solution. I just had to figure out how to be lovable!

I became obsessed, focused intently on being well-behaved: performing academically, being quiet, and playing nice. I had given myself a powerful distraction to shift my attention away from my powerlessness and place it on my responsibility to be the sort of little girl that could be lovable. I felt like I had saved myself; if I was careful enough, good enough, well-behaved enough they would love me, the fighting would stop and all would be well. My hope had been restored.

Unfortunately or fortunately, believing 'I'm unlovable' would play out like an old record in every area of my life. I couldn't see it until that fifth boyfriend broke up with me. The pain from that experience had tapped on this old wound; it emotionally jolted my awareness back to the circumstances which prompted me to unknowingly tell myself that lie. This pain was my invitation to reclaim my truth: in reality, there was no amount of good behaviour that was ever going to stop my parents from arguing. The truth was that I was powerless to stop my parents arguing and hurting one another, but - whether they could show me or not, I was lovable.

Pain is the fastest way our soul can call for our attention. The searing sensation from deep within is actually calling for our awareness. It's easy to see how we have all assumed that pain is bad, because it's so confusing. What is it asking us to do? What if it was asking for your attention?

For the majority of us, our emotional pain stems from our perceptions of certain experiences from when we were quite young. Between three and seven years old our inexperienced minds were quick to assume meanings or make judgements that seemed valid in the moment. We do this in an attempt to understand and grasp or comprehend otherwise confusing experiences. However, our young minds are often ill equipped to find supportive meaning for some of the challenging experiences we find ourselves in.

While they always tend to serve us for a time, there comes a point where the lie we once used to comfort and console ourselves creates more pain for us than it serves to mask. As we learnt about the world and tried to find our way safely through experiences, we turned to those around us to learn what was good, what was bad and what meant what. As adults we are now free to review these assumptions and judgements we've made about ourselves, and if any of the meaning we placed on past events are now causing us emotional pain, we are free to receive the truth and feel a liberating shift.

Heart Healing Magic

1)   Write below one recurring emotion showing up in your life. E.g. Anger, sadness, jealousy, guilt, frustration, dissatisfaction.

2)   Observe the pattern that has formed around that one particular feeling. Describe the pattern you can see as briefly as possible.

3)   Follow the pattern you have seen, back as far as you can to a clear memory of one of your earliest experiences with this pattern. Watch this memory like a movie playing on a screen, watch carefully and ask yourself, what did I make this mean? Use this memory to uncover the lie you told yourself that is now at the root of your recurring pattern.

Healing Affirmations

- That which hurts is untrue.

- My heartache will lead me to healing.

- I bravely face my heart wounds.

- I will listen to my pain.

- My reactions are my guide.

Chapter 4 –

Truth Heals

"*Healing may not be so much about getting better as about letting go of everything that isn't you. All of the expectations, all of the beliefs — and becoming who you are.*"

Rachel Naomi Remen

The perceptions we formed when we were young were helpful for a time, but now they are causing us more pain than they actually prevent. By acknowledging our heart wounds, we open to healing. Seeking heart healing is a process of seeking the truth from our higher power. It is only truth that can displace the lies we've believed for so long, and when you receive truth, you'll feel an unmistakable emotional shift. Truth feels good, and when you receive it your feelings will attest to the validity of what you've been told. Once this shift has taken place, it will alter and adjust every experience you manifest in life; because we manifest what we believe to be true. It is only when we have manifested evidence of this newly received truth that we are assured that true healing has taken place.

I was just about to leave to go to Japan for a university exchange. My dating spree had come to an end. And I was having less and less offers for dates as my time for departure drew nearer. I started seeing more of a friend named Binnie, someone who I had known socially for two years who I originally had a crush on. I had decided that he was too good for me when I first met him and purposely dropped my crush on him to avoid any disappointment.

Binnie's girlfriend had recently left to go overseas and as I was soon to likewise follow, we were both single, date-less and looking for company. He spontaneously asked me out; aware I was only a week away from my departure for Japan. I eagerly said yes, I was leaving soon and had nothing to lose. He picked me up and took me into Brisbane city for a surprise river boat cruise. In all of my dating experience, no one had ever been more generous or lavish, he had my attention.

While we had known each other for two years, it had only been a social friendship. This was the first night that we were actually alone together. As we sat there over dinner, he started sharing more about himself than I knew. It's like he just opened his whole heart to me, sharing his dreams, his fears and his hopes for the future.

I realised that while I had known him for two years, I didn't really know him at all. I sat back, absorbing everything he was sharing feeling incredibly comfortable and at peace in his presence. As the night unfolded, I felt myself emotionally feeling at 'home'. I was so disappointed that I had assumed this man was too good for me, and was suddenly aghast that I may have missed out on something incredibly special with him. He dropped me home after an incredibly enjoyable night out and asked if he could see me again the next day. I quickly responded, "yes", and returned inside very intrigued.

We met every day for the following five days before my departure flight over to Japan. Binnie was unlike any person I had ever dated before, he was open; he shared what he really thought and how he really felt. It was so comforting to not have to guess what was going on for him! He was so different to me; there was so much contrast in our personalities that it seemed to fit so well. Spending time with him was effortless, we didn't have to work on 'being' any way together. I finally felt free to just be who I was; after all I wasn't looking for love.

The night before I was leaving for Japan we were standing on my mother's porch in shock and grief. Our friendship and affection for each other had grown so quickly and the comforting feeling of home had pervaded every moment we shared together. I was awash with regret, and adamant that the prospect of love was not going to derail my plans for Japan. I told my heart to suck it up and forget about this random anomaly. I felt mournful the next day but intent on forgetting this strange experience and preparing for adventures in Japan.

Three years later, I was now living in Cairns and my mobile started ringing. I picked up, 'Hello, this is Lysa'; there was a very shy voice on the other end saying 'Hello'. Instantly I knew it was Binnie. I was so happy to hear his voice. I found out that he was living in New Zealand, and he told me he was interested in coming to Cairns and visiting me; I was awash with butterflies. He wasn't being clear, but I was sure through the lines I could hear his intentions.

His plane arrived the same day as a tsunami warning; I got into my car nonetheless, committed to swimming out to him if that's what it was going to take. I arrived at the domestic airport and waited, thinking carefully about where to stand so that I could catch the most flattering light. I was deep in thought considering what body language what would best represent my feelings toward him? Wondering whether I hugged him, kissed him or shook his hand upon arrival? Lost in the 'first contact' minutiae, I noticed the time for his arrival had passed; I was worried. I spoke to the customer service representative asking about the details of his flight and abruptly realised that he would be at the domestic terminal. Even though he was flying from New Zealand, he had changed flights in Brisbane.

Aghast, I began running, what if he was already there and thought I had stood him up? I didn't pause to think, I just ran as fast as I could, I was ten minutes away to the domestic terminal. Running in Cairns is the most perfect way to get hot, sweaty and end up with very frizzy hair, I was distraught! I still couldn't see him, and when he arrived I thought I would not look very appealing! I decided to stand and calm my beating heart. It's all alright, I said to myself, you are just as you are, if a bit of sweat and frizz can turn him off it will just make life all the easier! As I was calming myself looking afar off, Binnie walked into the terminal. He saw me before I realised he was there. I couldn't believe my eyes; there he was that guy I had dated for that one magical week all those years ago. It felt like no time had passed at all. He wrapped one arm around me and it felt so good. Something must have occurred in that moment, something must have clicked in or out of place, I'm not sure, but I instantly became a bumbling clumsy fool.

I walked to my car and returned to the pick-up zone, and helped him put his luggage in the boot. Then I tried to pull off in reverse; I giggled and blushed and shifted the gear stick into drive. But that was not the end; I had found Binnie accommodation in an apartment villa that I had lived in just a month prior. I was driving him to a place that I had just moved out from, and yet I passed by the driveway twice and had to reverse myself back to the entrance three times; blushing and giggling, I thought, oh my!

Then it was off to the supermarket to grab him some supplies. Tin after tin, apple after apple, I was dropping food. I was tripping over my feet and oblivious to all types of poles, obstruction and people in my way. Something had happened! And with my every blush, I sensed him blush too! There was unmistakable magic here that I could not deny.

Over the days and weeks we spent all of our spare time together. We would talk for hours, learning more about one another and finding ourselves increasingly at home with one another. I knew he wanted to propose, but I was definitely not ready for that conversation. I boldly spoke out and shared my fear, "I'm just not ready", I said, "Please don't ask me any important questions just yet." The whole time we were dating, my head and my heart were at war! I was hearing everything I wanted to hear from Binnie; I felt at home, the peace was immense, and yet my wounds spoke to me loudly, He'll leave you! They all leave you! No one would ever want to stay with you! I would shudder as the ego fear would cause me to retract and constrict.

I remember one day, we were walking through a gorgeous botanical garden in Cairns. I was in awe of the inherent beauty within the nature that surrounded me. My soul seemed to take over and I said to him, "I know we're meant to be together!" As soon as I heard what I'd said, I was gripped by anxiety! What did you just do?! I screamed at myself within. I escaped the moment by running to the toilet to breathe, I just wasn't ready for this I said to myself, so I returned meekly and lied in an attempt to take back my previous comments. "What I meant was, I know we are meant to be together for now." I felt his heart sink, I felt terrible seeing his disappointment.

Our courtship continued to flourish, more and more I received confirmation that he was my one. One night, while he was sitting close with his arm around me, I couldn't bear the pain anymore of trying to block the love coming from this man. I let the walls of my heart cave as I honestly said, "I'm afraid you'll leave me", and he responded, "I'll never leave you". I quickly retorted, "I don't believe you" and instantly he said, "That's ok, you will". The truth pierced my soul, as I finally felt like I could trust somebody to stay by my side. It was incredibly comforting to hear him acknowledge that it would take time for me to be able to believe him. He understood my pain, he knew my pattern; and he was prepared to show me his love until I could let my guard down and let him in.

In the moment he said "That's ok, you will", I knew I was worth staying with, I was lovable. I finally felt loved. As I shared my heart pain and my vulnerability with him, his love for me grew. He knew my fears and my doubts, and he chose to stay. In that moment when he said "That's ok, you will", a healing took place. I stopped resisting him and let his love in! We were married in Hamilton, New Zealand three months later.

For as long as I hold onto my own lies, I stay within the same familiar patterns of my past. I despise pain, I dislike it immensely and I'm willing to do anything in order to be free of it. What if being free of the pain actually meant telling ourselves the truth?

The truth comes to us as we deeply recognise the lie, and the pattern of pain it has caused. Truth feels expansive, it can arrive as an intuitive knowing or be delivered to us through angels, guides and messages from those around us.

As we use our pain to find the lies embedded in our souls, we give ourselves the opportunity to reclaim our truth. Truth heals us and opens us up to experiences in life that we've never known before.

Heart Healing Magic

1) Bring forward one lie that you uncovered from the previous chapter. Sit still, breath, pray and connect with your spiritual power and ask for the truth. Don't try and 'think' it; it will be revealed to you by a feeling, a whisper, a vision or a soul remembering.

2) Write down the newly found truth and use it as an affirmation for 7 days.

3) Watch and observe how your day unfolds differently now that you have reclaimed your truth. Write down below what changes you see in your world over the next seven days.

Healing Affirmations

- Truth brings me home to my heart.

- Truth is my sanctuary.

- I freely receive the truth.

- Truth envelopes me.

- Truth heals me.

Chapter 5 –

Emotion:

The Language

of the Soul

"Your intellect may be confused, but your emotions will never lie to you."

Roger Ebert

Our feelings are powerful messengers that seek to remind us of our truth and ask us to lovingly honour who we are. Our souls continually send us messages through our feelings, providing us with feedback on our choices in life. Many of us have been taught that certain feelings are bad to feel, causing us to unconsciously resist them. It's the feelings that we judge as being the most unacceptable that can end up permeating our daily lives. If left unacknowledged, our feelings can grow in intensity in a desperate bid to obtain our attention. I choose to see emotions as messengers, providing me with insight and valuable awareness.

It was another night of crippling anxiety for me. Anxiety is merely intense fear, a sensation that becomes more extreme and apparent the more adamantly we refuse to feel it. Once again, I was in the fridge stealing my flat mate's Brazil nuts. I had a pattern of stealing food from my flatmate as soon as I felt anxious; it was my way of trying to manage my emotional pain. The fat from its firm husk would melt away my momentary freak out and I could pretend that I was safe, content and satisfied for that tiny moment. After several late night anxiety driven nut stealing moments, I concluded that I was borderline insane. No, I was insane!

After shedding 12kg on an incredibly restrictive diet the previous year, I was still scared of food. I had finally shifted my last load of excess weight, and was a slim size 10. However, denying myself all of that delicious food I loved for so long had taken its toll, and compulsive binge eating was one of the consequences.

My bingeing had taught me not to permit myself any yummy foods in the house. So when I was gripped by anxiety late at night, I literally had nothing in the house that I could turn to for relief. One desperate anxiety filled night; I spied my flat-mates Brazil nuts hiding up on the back of the top shelf of the fridge. I thought, 'I'll just have a few and replace them in the morning'. But time after time, I would refill her nut supply, and then eat them later the same night. I watched as her jar of nutty goodness was becoming more and more obviously empty.

The thought of being busted stealing nuts, or being confronted about my nut stealing problem was utterly terrifying; actually scarier than my anxiety. This was my breakthrough! I wanted to maintain my image of being a 'Good-Girl' (p.s. good girls don't steal nuts) so much that I was willing to do something that I had never imagined doing before: To be with my anxiety and hear what it had to say. I walked away from the fridge in that moment, and retired to my room, with a sense of curiosity and commitment. "What did my anxiety have to say?" I wondered.

I didn't have to wait long before my anxious concerns floated to the surface, 'You're never going to find love', my anxiety shouted. 'Yes, well that may be true, or it may not. I still have a potential five decades on earth, so I could renounce my desire for love or continue to live in hope', I retorted to my anxiety. 'Yes, I DO want LOVE!' I exclaimed. My anxiety replied – 'BUT, where will I ever find him?' 'Well, we'll just have to hope that we'll bump into him somewhere', I calmly declared. 'But when I find him, he won't love me!' screamed my anxiety. Great, we had now shifted from never finding love, to finding Mr. Right and not being loved in return – I thought to myself, 'This is progress', and like a wise old woman I allowed my anxiety to dump her little concerns and frets about the unknown onto my loving lap as I assured her that no matter what she felt, I would listen. That night, through my powerful conversation with my anxiety I reached some new conclusions:

1. You can't know everything.

2. You can choose fear or faith.

3. You can make the unknown a fun adventure.

4. As I lovingly listen to my anxiety, it calms and soothes.

5. The more I listen to my fear the more compassion I have for myself and my human plight.

As we judge and disregard our feelings, we reject their value and cause them to escalate into demanding controlling sensations intent on forcing us to pay attention. Our emotions are unavoidable; we may be able to manage them with various mood-altering substances and experiences, namely: sex, food, shopping, gambling, alcohol, drugs, purging. Nevertheless, until we can embrace and receive all of our feelings for the inherent messages they bring, we will continue to feel powerless, trapped in an inescapable world of emotional volatility. As we lovingly listen to the messages our feelings bring, we can open up to their value and free ourselves to deepen into healing.

My anxiety taught me a powerful message - if I don't listen to my feelings then I force them to escalate in an attempt to gain my attention. The more of my loving attention and awareness I give to my feelings, the softer and easier they are to feel and understand.

Here are some of the feelings that I have resisted most in my life; including the messages they have brought me:

Anger

Anger lets me know that I have been disrespected, or that I have disrespected myself. It's so valuable to know I am angry, because it allows me to see that someone has crossed the line. If I can become aware and clear on how I've been disrespected, then I can improve my life by adjusting my personal boundaries. Being able to know how I deserve to be treated is essential for me to feel safe and calm. Anger shows me where to clarify my boundaries and when to defend them; it helps me make adjustments so that I can feel confident protecting myself.

My anger helps me to get clarity on the details of where my boundaries need to be. Being able to clearly communicate what is and what is not acceptable behaviour towards me feels empowering. The pain I feel when others disrespect my boundaries becomes my personal motivation to then go forward and more clearly communicate my boundaries to the people in my life. I know that I deserve to have people in my life who respect me, I feel strong and supported speaking up for myself.

Anger shows me where to clarify my boundaries and when to defend them; it helps me make adjustments so that I can feel confident protecting myself.

Jealousy

Jealousy lets me know that there is something I desire that I am denying myself. As soon as I feel jealous, I like to focus in on the details which have caused this feeling to surface: my friend's career success, my neighbour's haircut, or my sister's new car. By paying attention to my jealous feelings I can acknowledge what I desire for myself. Rather than feel bad about feeling jealous, I get excited knowing that I have the chance to discover what I do truly want for me.

When I realise that there are things or experiences that I yearn for, I can open up to potentially giving them to myself. The powerful message of jealousy has allowed me to open up more to who I really am. While I would like to 'think' that some things are not important to me, my jealousy actually clarifies to me whether or not this is really true. Jealousy therefore allows me to uncover what I truly treasure and value in life.

Jealousy therefore allows me to uncover what I truly treasure and value in life.

Sadness

Sadness lets me know that I have been disappointed or let down. It's the feeling that comes when I perceive the loss of someone or something in my life. Sadness is a powerful messenger that comes to show me when something I valued or sought after is no longer in my life. We cannot feel sad unless we've had something or someone in our lives that we treasured. I appreciate sadness for showing me the value of what I've had; it shows me what has been incredibly precious and sacred to me.

Sometimes I have taken experiences or people in my life for granted, and when they are not with me any longer it allows me to finally see the true worth they held for me. The clearer I am about what is truly valuable to me, the better I can choose tomorrow to fill my life with the same.

I appreciate sadness because it helps me to clarify what is truly valuable to me in this life.

Fear

Fear has become an informant ally for me in my life. I only feel fear when I attempt to control that which is outside of my control. For me, attempting to control my life had become second nature. Growing up in an emotionally volatile environment prompted an interesting response - I would try to read and recognise warning signs within my parents in an attempt to manage or manoeuver the situation towards a more favourable outcome than fighting. In an attempt to protect myself emotionally, I would try to read situations so that I could determine the outcome and prepare myself. Trying to know what was coming became my defense strategy and habitual response to life in general. I thought, 'If I know enough, I can prepare myself for what's coming or attempt to influence the situation to help myself.' Trying to know it all taught me a lot about people and their emotional responses, but inevitably there was information I couldn't access about my future that would terrify me.

Fear lets me know what is unknown. Fear taught me to recognise when I was allowing myself to be concerned with something that was outside of my sphere of influence. Fear was such an uncomfortable sensation for me that I allowed it to show me where I needed to let go. Fear showed me where I had no power, and taught me how to live in trust. It wasn't comfortable to begin with, but as I acknowledged that I didn't know something, I could open up to being with 'not knowing'. The longer I spent with 'not-knowing', the more I could see that I didn't need to know, life would continue to roll by and proceed irrespective of whether I knew what was going to happen or not. Without fear showing me where I couldn't 'control', I wouldn't have been able to develop my sense of trust with the continual unfolding of what is.

> ***Fear showed me where I had no power, and taught me how to live in trust.***

Our emotions are all incredibly valuable; they will not lie to us. They provide incredibly valuable information that can be used to help us craft a life that truly honours who we are. I would love to encourage you to be with your feelings more; to spend time with each of them and receive the valuable insights they are offering you. I assure you that the more time you spend paying attention to your feelings, the easier it will become to understand what they want you to know.

Imagine if we could harness the insight from our feelings to make adjustments in our daily lives? Using the insight gleaned from our daily feelings could help us create a richer, more fulfilling experience of life. Giving yourself permission to feel and flow through whatever feelings are present, will become your doorway to freedom. As Robert Frost shares, "The best way out is always through." Allowing yourself to deepen into connecting with yourself and receiving your feelings is a precious, loving, life changing investment in yourself.

Heart Healing Magic

1)   Name that one feeling that you have been resisting most today.

2)   Look at how often that one feeling has been coming up over the recent days, months or years.

3)   Listen to what this feeling has to share with you. What message is your soul sending to you through this one feeling?

Healing Affirmations

- I hear my soul.

- I listen with love.

- I am brave being with all of my feelings.

- My feelings guide me.

- I choose to feel.

Chapter 6 –

Two Halves

Form the Whole

"The deeper that sorrow carves into your being, the more joy you can contain."

Khalil Gibran

When we try to like some parts of life and not all of life, we are asking life to continually show us the parts we don't like; or as Carl Jung taught, 'What we resist persists.' There cannot be love without fear, for we can only know one by the presence of another. Opening up to see the composite of all, frees us to ease into what is and appreciate the inherent value of every part. Whatever we experience is just one part of a great whole.

It was time! Binnie and I had been married for two years, and suddenly we felt like someone was missing. We knew it was time to open up to receive a baby. I couldn't believe that I'd conceived within a matter of weeks. I remember the joy, the lightness and awareness swell within me. I had known for a few years that I was intuitive, but suddenly I felt my gift multiply in strength. I was receiving so much information. My husband was in awe; he needed to test my capacity and took me to a busy area at church where I knew very few people, (He'd lived in the area ten years prior and was very familiar with the people there). When he saw someone whose background he knew, he would ask me what their occupation was. Over and over again I was bang on, intuitively guessing correctly; he was in shock and so was I.

We had a feeling our little baby was a boy, and instantly felt his name was 'Melchizedek'; the name of a great high priest from the scriptures. I knew he was a powerful spirit and felt joy considering what would change for us all as he entered our world. His presence had heightened my intuitive awareness and enhanced my empathy. Days and weeks passed joyfully, I was beautifully naive about pregnancy.

My breasts and appetite grew quickly. It was time for my eight week scan, and because Binnie was busy as a shift-worker doing four twelve hour shifts consecutively, I decided to go on my own rather than delay the appointment. The scan proceeded as normal; I had no idea what the purpose of the scan was as I lay back unpresuming. "Hmm, I'm not quite able to get a heartbeat", the radiographer said, "Baby must still be too small. Let's book another appointment in a week, and see if we can get a heartbeat then."

The radiographer said our baby was 'too small' for her to register the heartbeat, but I had felt differently over the last few days. Something had changed. I returned home quiet, still. I waited for Binnie to come home as I told him what had happened; we both had a sense of what would soon be confirmed.

Two days later, I had a visit from my sister-in-law, she was congratulating me on our new baby, but I was reluctant to share her joy. She was accompanied by a friend who happened to be a midwife, and I started asking about the signs of miscarriage. I sat calmly as she explained, and my heart sank with recognition, I knew he was gone. The next thing I remember was waking up to a crippling pain that felt like menstruation multiplied by five! It was final confirmation and my heart sank further with the evidence that my body was releasing him, my little baby boy.

My husband was equally devastated by our loss; we had never known such joy since being brought together. The thought of a little being coming through our love had lifted us to new found bliss. So, in equal compensation for the joy we had felt, we plummeted into a new depth of sadness that we had never known before. For four days we cried; we cried eating together, we cried watching movies, and eventually we decided to cry into the garden, hopeful that our outpouring could nourish the soil and potentially aid the growth of some new life.

We prayed and felt that our little boy would always be with us, this truth was incredibly comforting. Nevertheless we both knew that it was still time to bring new life into our family. We consulted with our local doctor who warned us against another pregnancy so soon, stating that the trauma to my body would be unproductive for a successful pregnancy. We considered his warning, but still we couldn't ignore the prompting to bring life forward. We decided to stick with our inspiration and refuse contraception; we waited open and receptive to conceive once more.

Within six weeks I had conceived again, but I didn't acknowledge the pregnancy until I was five weeks in. I decided to take a test, and the confirmation weighed on my heart. Yes, we were pregnant again, but for how long… The days and weeks passed slowly. I refused to connect with my baby; the fear of loss had crippled me. This time, my husband was sure to accompany me to the eight week scan. They confirmed a heartbeat and I was relieved, but still apprehensive and unwilling to allow this child into my heart.

I had never known loss like losing Melchizedek. During our second pregnancy, I remained frozen in a constant state of fear. I didn't allow myself to get too happy for fear of the devastating loss reoccurring. While my husband and I were walking one day, we started playing with boy's names. We had to go through the alphabet, one letter at a time and suggest a name starting with that letter: A – Andrew, B – Brett, C – Cameron… As we progressed through to U, I said – Union… both of us stopped walking and said, "wait on that's close" and then Binnie said "Orion!" Both of us felt the soar of elation in our hearts as it was confirmed that that was his name.

We never entertained another option and as we began speaking with him, singing to him and telling him stories, our love for Orion grew. He always kicked and wriggled when I was in the bath, he obviously enjoyed the sensation of buoyancy as we floated there together. At 35 weeks, I had a bath and he wasn't moving; I quickly panicked getting out of the bath calling to my husband. We poked him, called out his name and I moved around as much as I could to 'wake' him from his supposed slumber. Nothing! I phoned the midwife and asked her to come quickly, she arrived within minutes and we swiftly used the Doppler machine to confirm a gentle rhythmic heartbeat; he had just been asleep.

I realised that our little Orion had called my bluff; it was only when I thought I might have lost him that I realised he already had my heart. I had compassion for my sensitive soul, our loss of Melchizedek was still so fresh, but I didn't want to dishonour Orion by refusing to bond with him now. Whether he would come forward or move onward without us; I wanted my baby to feel welcomed, loved and accepted within me. From that hour, I gave myself permission to fall deeply in love with Orion, whatever the outcome.

Time passed quickly and soon I was in the hospital receiving him into my arms. His little blue eyes and fair curly hair astonished me. As he squinted and strained to open his eyes, he locked gaze with me as love washed through us both. I could feel a depth of love between us that my mind couldn't comprehend. The connection, recognition and bond I felt with this little soul filled me with ecstasy. It was pure bliss to see him and realise that he too was deeply in love with me, his mother. Once we retired to a private room to settle for our first night together, I laid him down in the bassinet and gave thanks for this little child. I prayed for peace to be upon me, as I rested from my role of housing Orion's growing body and asked that Melchizedek be assigned an angel to watch over and protect his little brother.

From that moment, the fear, anxiety and constant worry of losing my baby vanished. I knew he would be safe, and that his big brother was elated being able to learn and grow by watching Orion's experiences here on earth.

Losing our first baby Melchizedek showed us the depth of love that we had for him; the sadness we felt was confirmation that he had been truly dear and precious to us, even though we shared but eight short weeks with him. On the other side, receiving our second son was such an elation and joy that it made our loss complete. The depth of our pain and loss with Melchizedek became equal to our capacity to hold new joy with Orion.

Life is one great continuum of duality, sometimes we experience one side, other times we experience the other. The greatest advantage of duality is that it allows us to gain clarity through contrast:

- Without illness we cannot value health.

- Without suffering we cannot value pleasure.

- Without sorrow there can be no joy.

- Without heartbreak, we cannot value the reciprocation of love.

- Without loneliness we cannot appreciate connection.

- Without fear we cannot know love.

Heart Healing Magic

1) Recall an experience that you have labelled as 'bad'. How did that experience also bless your life?

2) Think of a feeling that you have considered 'bad', and recall a time recently when you felt that feeling. What message is that feeling bringing to you?

3) Bring forward one individual whom you feel hurt you. Think of them, and feel the resistance toward them. How have they helped you? How did their actions actually bring blessings into your life?

Healing Affirmations

- I see all things as whole.

- With one comes the other.

- I open to see both parts in all.

- Everything emanates for one complete whole.

- I see unity in all things.

Chapter 7 –
Giving Forgiving

"Forgiveness is just another word for Freedom."

Byron Katie

Forgiveness should really be called 'releasing'; the act of forgiving is actually a process of releasing ourselves from judgement. In the moment we attempt to tie others with our judgements, we unconsciously bind ourselves. When we judge another we feel has wronged us, we think we can brand them as: bad, unworthy or undeserving. Our judgements of others take no effect in their lives, but instead stay with us. When we refuse to forgive, we refuse to free ourselves from the judgements we thought we had assigned to another

The love that I saw on my mother's side of the family was based in fear and a need to control. I was taught and shown that in order to receive love, you needed to conform to the authority present. When I lived in-line with their wishes, I had their attention and affection. If I disagreed or spoke out I would face the silent treatment; the withdrawal of love. This was my punishment for having my own opinion and desires; for disapproving of their ways.

My nana had been raised by a woman who refused to love her own child. I never really knew my great nana, but I knew she must have had her own pain, her own reasons for rejecting her first born child. My nana had never felt cared for, important or valued. She fell pregnant, conceiving a child outside of wedlock and promptly married young; her chance to escape from the unloving home she'd been raised in. She had been emotionally motherless and now found herself, a mother.

Nana had shared how painful it was for her to be ignored by her own mother, and yet over the years, if her children did not conform to her ideas, she would shut them out in exactly the same way. She had two brothers, who in contrast enjoyed a good relationship with their mother. It must have been very confusing and cutting to see your own mother reject and mistreat you, while being kind and loving towards your own siblings.

I found it all fascinating, what shame did my great nana live with? What would prompt her to emotionally abandon her own child? These questions would go unanswered. As I got older, this pattern of fear based love became more apparent to me. When nana disapproved of any choices that her children made, she would stop talking to them. They would receive fewer gifts at Christmas, and fewer invitations to spend time with her. I was astonished to see that the suffering that my nana had received would become the very same punishment she would choose for her own children.

Nana's first born child, the one born out of wed-lock, was my mother. This pattern would become incredibly significant in my own life. If I was obedient and dutiful, I would stay in good rapport. Mum and I would talk together, have fun and feel like 'friends'; but, if I failed to fulfill expectations, everything would change. When I didn't conform, Mum would simply stop talking to me. I would ask questions, and be met with silence. Until I adjusted my behaviour or apologised, I would face being shut out.

I had pity for the suffering of these women in my life, and yet I abhorred their choice to perpetuate the pain by passing it on. Withdrawing love had always been a powerful way to force conformity in our family; and it got results. As this pattern of control became more evident to me, my resentment towards it grew. I was committed to ending this pattern in my life.

I remember talking to a friend, sharing my distain for my family's generational pattern of fear-based control. She responded, 'Well, why do you do this to yourself?' I sat in shock, horrified; I too, was still keeping the tradition alive. I observed how I would disconnect from myself whenever I failed to meet my own expectations. I would stop listening to myself, and actually shut myself out; I would withhold my own love and care from myself when I was scared or locked in self-judgment. It dawned on me that the behaviours that we judge and condemn in others, lie waiting within us. The things we find most abhorrent, can stay within us until we reach a level of fear, anxiety or powerlessness and then boom – out they come to play, replaying the old pattern once more. Witnessing how wounds are passed on from one generation to the next was monumental for me; I vowed to heal and break the cycle.

It dawned on me that the behaviours that we judge and condemn in others, lie waiting within us.

I began to see how our judgement of others, does little to alter their behaviour. Instead, as we judge others we actually allow their behaviour to sink deep into our own soul. Fear becomes the trigger, which causes us to reach down into what we have judged the worst in others, and bring it forward as punishment for those who will not heed to our will. For years I practiced having compassion for myself, I recognised that my emotional awareness was the key to being able to stay with myself when I wanted to shut myself out. Nevertheless, even as I saw my own behaviour towards myself improve, I could still sense the depth of anger, pain and judgment within me that I held towards my mum and nana. I had always ignored themes on 'forgiveness'; assuming that only the purest most noble souls would be capable of cleansing themselves of the judgements they harboured towards another. I thought that forgiveness was all about cleaning the slate in order to recreate or resume a more loving relationship with someone; but it was my own self-sabotage and my own self-rejection that called me to forgive.

I felt inspired to write a letter, to pour out my heart to my nana, and share my pain with her. To share my experience of the pattern of our family and say that I forgave her, and that I too was sorry. I was sorry for making her behaviour bad as she had made her mother's behaviour bad. I let her know how much I loved her and how much her example had strengthened me. I spoke into the noble, honourable part of my nana that I adored. The truth of who she was, and realised that we are not our behaviours, we are not the cruel things we do, we are not the generational pain we have observed all our lives. I developed compassion for her; I empathised with her blindness and saw myself. As I released my judgement against my nana, it was the weight that lifted off my own heart that would prove the most profound. I felt a healing take place as I removed judgment from my mum, my nana and my great nana.

As I released my judgement against my nana, it was the weight that lifted off my own heart that would prove the most profound.

I realised that when we judge a behaviour, we actually allow it to nestle into a quiet dark space within us, and when our own desperation or powerlessness calls on a weapon that will be best equipped to avenge us, we will turn to this 'bad' judged part within ourselves. Forgiving my mother and my nana and my great nana had nothing to do with improving my relationship with any of them. It was all about improving my relationship within myself, and releasing my pattern.

Our judgements of others unconsciously becomes our own self-imposed prison, we end up wearing the 'bad', 'unworthy' and 'undeserving' labels. Forgiving brings freedom, not for those we judged, but for ourselves! The key to forgiveness is remembering that what we give unto others, we give to ourselves. The process of releasing another from our judgement allows us to consciously recall the bonds we thought we inflicted upon them, and observe the ties loosen as we free ourselves.

Forgiving brings freedom, not for those we judged, but for ourselves!

Heart Healing Magic

1)   Bring forward the person you despise the most in your life right now. Write a list consciously recalling every judgment you have placed on that person.

2)   Write down the feelings you can feel as you read this list of judgments.

3)   Pray and ask for guidance to support you to release these judgements from the person in question and yourself.

Healing Affirmations

- I release them and set myself free.

- I free myself from suffering; I forgive them.

- I bravely release my judgement; I release my pain.

- I breathe into forgiveness.

- I love you, I forgive you, I'm sorry, thank you.

Chapter 8 –

Heart's Desire:

The True Compass

LYSA BLACK

"And no heart
has ever suffered
when it goes in search
of its dream."

Paulo Coelho

While we may have no proof that what we desire exists, the yearning we feel from within our heart beckons to us continually, inviting us to seek out that which we dream of. It is only our unhealed wounds from the past which prevent us from acknowledging our hearts desires. Unveiling the truth of what we yearn for connects us to the courage we all need to pursue our dreams. What if the desires in your heart were the beacons calling you to your soul path?

I had bravely realised that the rejection I perceived from my boyfriends was actually coming from within me. When I packed up and left Brisbane I moved with a commitment to learn to love myself! Whatever that meant? I decided it would mean: To embrace all of myself on the physical, emotional, mental and spiritual levels. I can remember arriving at the airport in Cairns without having any accommodation planned. I had always lived a planned, organised life and never allowed myself to live spontaneously. And phew what a rush of relief to arrive and know that I only had to choose my next step in the very moment that I saw the next step appear.

I had bravely realised that the rejection I perceived from my boyfriends was actually coming from within me.

At the airport foyer I glanced over the accommodation options and my heart sang at one place on the main esplanade. I used one of the free phones there to call and asked to be picked up. Wow, they actually came and picked me up; I felt like a Princess being escorted to her new palace. I still had a few thousand dollars up my sleeve and I decided that I was going to honour myself by choosing work that I would enjoy. Work that would light me up. I set an intention to find work within two weeks and promptly went to lie in the sun.

Being spontaneous was freeing, it was smooth. In the past I would fret and worry about what I didn't know, and now the many unknowns before me felt like a magical mystery all unfolding in perfect timing. I took up yoga classes, made time to be lazy and when the feeling came, I would get dressed up in one of my favourite dresses and strut the streets waiting for my heart to lead me onward. I would turn left, when I felt to turn left, I absolutely paid attention to every internal whim as though it was the most perfect internal compass available. I had sales experience; I spoke fluent Japanese, there were so many options available. I would go into a shop and take a look to see if I liked the feel of it, I would talk with the owner to see if they had any staffing needs. There was plenty of interest and if any opportunity felt good I'd dip my toe in to feel it out more. Intuitively I kept hearing "No", there were so many jobs that I could do, but none that made my heart sing and I was committed to hold out for what my heart would bellow out for. I needed it, desperately. Everything I had thought was true and reliable had let me down. It was time to truly deeply, honestly and always trust my own heart and do whatever I had to in order to find my joy.

It was a Saturday afternoon, I decided to take the day off from searching for work and instead went searching for special places in Cairns that I would love. I turned down a corner and saw a dress shop with a huge window. In the front there was a gorgeous display of underwear, mannequins, fancy racing hats and art deco calendars, "Go – There!", My heart called, I almost felt my feet rush ahead and as soon as I crossed the threshold of the doorway my whole body was awash with warmth and tingles. I didn't know if it was seeing so many beautiful dresses in one place, the amber low-lighting, or the Janis Joplin music in the background, but I knew in that moment that this was where I wanted to work.

It was amazing, it truly was the dress shop of my dreams! The owner was busy serving and I was shocked to think my heart wanted… to sell dresses?! I stumbled out of the shop, in awe of what I had just experienced and as I moved down the street I found another dress shop and felt prompted to once again go in. I liked it, but it didn't grab my soul like before. This shop wasn't as busy and I started asking the attendant about 'Tea Lily', the dress shop I had just left. I said I had fallen in love with it and wanted to work there. She listened to me gush for a while and then shared that the lady working over in that shop also owned the shop I was in. This attendant said she may be interested in meeting me. Wow, I wondered if everything would now be paved out beautifully for me, just as a reward for daring to follow my own heart.

I was told to go into Tea lily on a Monday when there would be fewer customers and sure enough C.V. in hand and decked out in my favorite dress, I walked into the shop and introduced myself. The owner received me in such a graceful welcoming manner, I instantly felt at home. She asked if I had time for an interview straight away, "Of course", I said. We sat down in the back section of her shop and within minutes she was offering me a full-time position to work in her gorgeous dress shop. I was sold; this 'trusting your heart' stuff totally works!

It was such a joyful experience for me to be able to receive employment in a place that lit up my soul. During my time at Tea Lily I flourished, every day I got to dress up, love myself and talk to women about beautiful dresses and how they could help themselves to look and feel their most gorgeous! Living in Cairns taught me that when I sat in my soul and honoured the desires of my heart, I could open to beautiful new experiences which filled my life with more love than I had known. When we live in our soul, it is easy to expand into whatever we desire; this experience helps us to feel safer, calmer, more trusting, more open and receptive. We are no longer ruled by a long list of fears, but we connect with a part of ourselves that is expansive, which is just a constant beautiful unfolding and unfurling. Healing is not just about finding a way out of pain, it is about finding our way to our most enriching, fulfilling and satisfying life possible. What we want is not an ironic mirage mocking us cruelly, the sincere desires of our hearts are the beacon to our most fulfilling future.

Healing is not just about finding a way out of pain, it is about finding our way to our most enriching, fulfilling and satisfying life possible.

Heart Healing Magic

1) Use this page to write down everything that your heart longs for. It can be words, feelings, experiences, miracles, outcomes, people or animals. Go wild, let your pen run free and list what your heart longs for.

2) Re-read over your list above and pay close attention to how you feel as you read each word. Pay attention to the words that make your heart sing, vibrate or glow. Circle the one desire that brings you the biggest buzz, and allow it to be the desire that now leads you forward.

3) Now that you have identified one sincere heart desire, write down the messages and feelings that are coming from your ego. There will be a story that it brings forward to show you all the reasons why you can't have what you want. Write down the reasons your ego tells you that you can't have what you want. (These will be wounds that are ready to be healed).

Healing Affirmations

- I heed the call from my heart.

- My heart is my compass.

- I hear my heart and honour its call.

- My heart is my sanctuary.

- What I long for, longs for me.

Chapter 9 —
Ego: The
Shadow Compass

LYSA BLACK

"*Fear is the natural reaction to moving closer to the truth.*"

Pema Chodron

Ego is a protective function within our mind, it attempts to shield us from suffering. It was born when we were born and activates once we experience discomfort and pain. The intention of our ego is to keep us safe; it monitors what we experience and concludes beliefs based on our responses. If our ego believes that certain people or experiences will bring us pain, then it concludes that they are dangerous; this is where our desire for pleasure and hatred of pain comes from. Our ego guides us to experiences that will bring us pleasure, and tells us to run away from anything that will bring us pain. The problem with trusting our ego to judge a situation is that the only information that it has to make conclusions, are our own past experiences.

My ego is incredibly harsh; it is self-righteous, arrogant, selfish, stingy and judgemental. It attempts to puppeteer my choices in life by feeding me a list of 'There isn't enough', 'You must...', and 'Don't let them see who you really are!' My healing journey opened me up to realise that I am not my ego; I am the soul within. As I would seek after the desires of my heart the berating, intimidation and fear that ensued would debilitate me. My woe is me story: 'My mummy doesn't love me' was the pinnacle of its creation. A strap-line that would ensure my compliance, my ego had convinced me that no one in the world had my back that I had to make it on my own, be tough and look after myself. Every time that I would seek after a desire in my heart, my ego would only have to throw at me, 'But even your mum doesn't love you. So, you can't do that!' and the game was over; I would surrender and submit.

My healing journey opened me up to realise that I am not my ego; I am the soul within.

After being intuitively taught these amazing principles of self healing I began to recognise how my ego would intimidate me and scare me away from the dreams in my heart; and it all came down to my woe is me story: 'My mumma don't love me'. This story seemed so real to me, that I felt powerless to negotiate with my ego; I knew I needed help. Although I had been coaching other people to miraculous results for six years, this story had me blindsided. I couldn't wriggle it on my own. I was intuitively guided to a coach in Canada who I knew in my heart had the power to shake me free! I reached out to her, and asked for help. It wasn't long before we had a series of coaching sessions set up, I knew healing was coming because the level of resistance I had to doing this work with her was monumental; it was perfect confirmation!

When we started working together, I expected her to ask me to: forgive my mum, love my mum, and heal my relationship with her. However, she knew the true source of my wound; my relationship with myself. She set me a personal challenge to write an anonymous love letter every day for 21 days. My task was to pour into a love letter all of the love that I wished I had been given by my mum as a little girl. She taught me that 'What we give unto others, we give to ourselves'; and I knew it was true. Each day I would wake up and pour the love I wished I had received into a letter. I would address the letter: 'To you', and sign off, 'From a friend' I placed the love letter into an unmarked envelope and would keep it with me during the day, waiting for my heart to tell me who it was meant for. I accepted her challenge and writhed in ego resistance, hearing 'How's giving what I didn't get going to help me!' – I knew it confirmed it would be a valuable practice for me.

She taught me that 'What we give unto others, we give to ourselves'; and I knew it was true.

According to my agreement with my coach I delivered love letters for 21 days, to 21 individuals. Sometimes, I would drop one off in a letterbox, or give it to someone to pass to someone else to ensure my anonymity. Other days I would walk straight up to a stranger, pull the letter out from my handbag and say "This is for you". The reactions were completely unique every time, some people would say "Thank you", others would say "No Thank you", some would put it in their pockets and others would run back towards me after reading it, fling their arms around my body and hug me tighter than I have ever experienced before.

Every day that I would pour love into those letters for myself, I would step through another level of resistance to giving myself love. As I invested myself diligently into giving, I truly felt the power of receiving in my life. One lady was having lunch and I handed her the letter just as I walked out, moments later she returned sobbing asking how I knew, "You wouldn't believe what happened to me yesterday" she shared, with tears streaming down her eyes she said "Thank you" in a way that penetrated my heart.

One night I was delaying my delivery, I had seen so many miraculous experiences and my ego was saying, "You've done enough, yeah it works alright, stop now". I felt myself succumbing but this helped me to see how imperative this one love letter was for me that night, I knew the letter was significant. It talked about how I could see the hard work and effort that this person invested in those around him. I acknowledged his loving heart and his noble spirit.

I jumped into the car just as the sun was setting; it was a Friday night and I knew my love letter recipient would be on the walkway of a nearby street. I listened to my soul, I knew where to go and there I saw him: A young Maori man with a white singlet on, jeans hung low, baseball cap twisted on his head. Instantly I knew it was for him, and my ego stepped in, "Look at him, he's not noble. He's about to go drinking for the night, and he only cares about himself" This confirmed that it was for him, and I felt nervous. I pulled my car up next to him and wound down my window. I waved to him from the sidewalk and held out the precious love letter in my hand. He casually walked over and bent down to my window. His smiled gleamed into my car and as I looked at him I truly saw his noble soul. His smile was pure and genuine, his loving heart was evident and it seemed to me for that moment that he was wearing shining armor. I said, "This is for you. It's a love letter", and he reached out and took it into his hand with so much appreciation and thanks that I was struck! Struck to see the error of my ego's false conclusion of his nature! That was it; I saw that I had mistakenly judged myself.

That was it; I saw that I had mistakenly judged myself.

What I realised through this powerful process was that the judgments I held about myself, I held against everyone. As I genuinely invested myself in loving them, I saw how truly lovable they really are and it was the evidence I needed to finally see my own lovability. The most common response to my letters was "Why?" The beaming smiles, hugs and profuse gratitude filled up my soul, aligning me with my truth: I am love.

Many of us mistakenly believe that we are our ego. That all of the thoughts we hear in our mind are ours. The truth is that there are two key parts to your identity. One part was born at your birth, activated by suffering, it's the dialogue that identifies threats and constantly dialogues about how to get more pleasure and avoid pain. The other aspect of your identity is your soul; your soul existed before your birth and it will survive past your death. It's the part of you that is here seeking learning, growth and expansion. It's the part that contains your gifts, talents, desires, intuition and the part that is capable of connecting to everyone and spirit.

Ego is limited, it trusts nothing and it can't connect. It only knows itself as separate, singular and alone. Its objective is to survive in the most pleasant way possible. Our ego attempts to gain control of us by having us believe that:

1. We are our ego.

2. That we are only our separateness, our aloneness.

3. That we are only our body.

4. That we are only alive until death.

5. That we must seek out security, safety and our own needs.

Living from ego disconnects us from the expansion, sureness and love that always surround us. Our ego gains control over our soul as it distracts us with concerns about how we can get what we want, and how we can avoid experiencing the things that have hurt us in the past. The clearest way to discern ego is by feeling its desperate, forceful attempt to need, get, become. When we are thinking from ego, it's always a must! Our ego insists upon our compliance; the feeling of force and fear is debilitating. It makes us feel small and threatens us with our incredibly restrictive, albeit familiar woe is me story.

Rather than back down and stay within the confinement of what I knew, I decided to start seeing my ego talk as a kind of false indicator of what I could do. When its familiar criticism began, I started adjusting myself to acknowledge that if my ego really didn't want me to do something, then it was a sign that I needed to do it. Our ego can only argue what it knows and as soon as we venture into unknown waters, it gets scared that we will align closer and closer with our soul; and it will have less power and influence in our lives, Once I realised that there are only two choices: To follow my ego or follow my soul, I realised that if my ego didn't like my suggested plan, then it was perfect. This allowed my ego dialogue to become particularly valuable to me. Every time ego screamed "No", I got excited, because it really meant – "Yes!" from my soul.

Once we form our first ego conclusions; our very capacity to view the world is altered so that we can only see a reflection of what we believe to be true. Being able to identify your ego is a powerful path to healing; it will most clearly show you what needs to be healed. When we live under the control of our ego we can only see the refracted perspective of what we've believed to be true. Thus our eyes are basically tainted and limited, incapable of seeing the truth of the world around us. We become victims to our own ego, allowing it's judgements to affect our decision making. It is only through healing that we can receive the truth and light to be able to correctly perceive the world and make choices based on the truth of who we know ourselves to be.

Ego resistance truly is the most perfect way to know you are on the right track. I always remind myself that there is nothing within me that I cannot face. If it is within me, it is only a fragment of a past experience that I have survived. Even the most horrific and painful experiences of our past are experiences that we been able to endure! It takes focus and time to play with your shadow compass, but the path that will open up before you as a result, is magnificent. You will open up to love, friendship, experiences and magic that you have never known. You will finally align with your soul in a way that will bring what you desire into your life. You will be filled will a new found peace and joy that comes from living a life that honours your soul.

Heart Healing Magic

1) Give your ego a name; is it male or female, young or old?

2) Write a letter to your ego expressing your gratitude for all the ways that it has protected you over your lifetime. Thank it for its intention to keep you safe and away from harm. Tell your ego that you really appreciate its perspective and that you want to continue to hear its view but from now on you will also be consulting with your soul/intuition.

3) Bring forward a current decision that needs to be made in your life. Write down all of the ego fears and concerns. Intently listen to all of the concerns it has, they are valid. Next use a new sheet of paper, and ask your soul/spirit/higher-self for its perspective. Choose to consider both sides, and feel into what will be the best choice for you right now.

Healing Affirmations

- I am not my wounds.

- My Soul speaks peace; my ego speaks fear.

- Deep into the unknown I go, heedless to the ego call.

- Resistance marks my true path.

- On the other side of resistance, my freedom awaits.

Chapter 10 – The World is our Mirror

"As above so below,

as within so without."

Author Unknown

'Transnoia' means, seeing everything in life as a call to learning and healing. It's allowing ourselves to see everything as a lesson and a blessing. Our ego tries to convince us that the world is an unkind and unloving place, but as I have sought to use everything I encounter in life as a call-to-healing; healing has manifested itself. The greatest value in being able to look out into the world is that we can in turn begin to see within ourselves more clearly. It's only when we have eyes to see within that we can open to our healing journey.

I had just given birth to my little girl Bow a few months prior; she was around three or four months old when I was finally able to sleep through the night again. By this stage I was thoroughly sleep deprived and exhausted. It was around this time that there was one special night that would invite me to look deeper into myself. Everyone in the house was asleep, except me. I was in so much of a pattern of waking regularly at night to feed Bow that I was finding it hard to sleep; I was getting myself more and more annoyed, which was making it less and less likely that I even could sleep. So there I was lying wide awake, annoyed at the calm silence that taunted me. Suddenly I heard a kitten meow. It was right under my bedroom window. I lay there surprised, waiting for Binnie to stir from the noise. Alas, he slept on and my maternal instincts knew the kitten's cry was one of desperation and need. I thought, I don't want to take care of someone else's baby right now! My baby is sleeping and I want to be asleep too. The cry from the kitten increased in frequency and intensity, and I knew it knew I could hear it.

I remember observing how much resistance I felt to offering care to that cat. I wanted to believe that I didn't care because it was not my responsibility. My tender heart lured me out of bed and I walked to the front door to meet this little one. Peering out into the dark feeling annoyed, I saw this little scruffy tabby and felt my heart swoon and rush with love, my kindness had returned. As I got closer, the kitten drew nearer in trust and I was able to see how dirty, skinny and obviously hungry it was. It certainly did need my help. I went to get some milk, a cardboard box and a towel for warmth.

In the morning I knew that this kitten was a little messenger for me; the wide array of strong emotions and the high level of resistance was confirmation. I continued to ask myself, what is this cat trying to show me? The following morning my husband and I decided we were not ready for a pet, and it would need to be taken to an animal shelter. Once that was concluded it started off an emotional cascade within me: sadness, powerlessness, and anger swirled around violently within. I gasped finally allowing myself to see how the kitten was reflecting my 'unwantedness'. It had been drawn towards me, intent on showing me how I had felt about myself for so many years.

I became increasingly distraught as I drove the lost kitten to the animal shelter; I was no longer concerned for the kitten who I knew would receive care, but I was worried for my own plight. I was overwhelmed allowing myself to now witness my own past pain. Prior to getting married, I had been plagued by the feelings of deep sadness, loss, disappointment and anger. I had never been starved, or left out in the cold, but emotionally I believed that no one was there for me when I was younger; there was no care for me in sight. How do I now care for myself, so long after I actually needed help? I sobbed and sobbed as I drove with a friend to the animal shelter; I must have looked ridiculous!

Only days later, there was a knock at the door, and I was face-to-face with two police officers and a young Maori man in his early 20's. Instantly I felt confused and frightened, the police asked me if I knew this young man in front of me. I admitted that I had never seen him before. He asked if the previous owners of our house still lived here and I informed him that they did not. Once that was confirmed, the police said, "Come along then" to the young man, and all of a sudden I realised what had happened. For whatever reason this young man was misplaced, with nowhere to go; if I had known him he would have been able to stay here with me instead of being taken away by the police. Realising that this young man was also unwanted, lost and abandoned jabbed at my exposed heart wound. I shut the door and fell into a pool of tears. There I was again, 'unwanted', 'abandoned'! I had manifested another clear reflection of a wound I had long denied.

A few months later I was visiting my in-laws out in the country. At night the stars are so bright out there that they feel closer than usual. While there one night I had the distinct impression to run a deep bath and get in with the lights out. I immediately ran the bath. As soon as I entered the bath, I sank deeply into the warm water surrounding me up to my chin; I had the distinct impression that I was back inside the womb. When I imagined myself there tucked inside my mother's womb, I recalled feeling unwanted. I think that was when this wound was formed; as a little babe I had concluded that I was unwanted. As soon as I thought this, sharp shuddering pain surfaced and moved though my whole body. The pain was showing me that what I had long believed was not true. I looked up through the nearby window to see a myriad of bright stars. Right then, a vision opened up to me there in the dark. I was shown a concord of beautiful shining angels full of light, they were all singing and rejoicing, acknowledging my entrance to this world.

The pain was showing me that what I had long believed was not true.

The truth washed through my being as I realised that I was meant to be. Those angels knew me, and they were joyful at my arrival. From that moment on I knew I had healed that wound. Rather than believe I was unwanted, I could now see my truth; that I was divinely intended. I felt a new sense of purpose and belonging, and I have not seen any reflections of 'unwanted' since.

The symbol, experience or person that taps on our wounds is

not what is most important to observe. It's the emotional response that comes, which provides the most valuable information. The intense feelings that surface will actually allow you to travel back through your memories and reconnect with a pain that you have assumed is long since gone and forgotten. The feelings and thoughts you have in these moments of reaction are incredibly precious, you will need them to guide you back to the genesis of the wound; that which is asking to be healed.

Receiving the truth is a pivotal step in heart healing; it's imperative because if we do not reclaim our truth, then we remain stuck in our lie. In this example I was remembering my self-imposed label of 'I'm unwanted'; the unwanted kitten and the unwanted Maori man were showing me this reflection of what I thought of myself. Everything around you is a powerful reflection, showing you more of yourself and it's our emotional reactions to what we see that become valuable insights helping us to identify and eventually heal our wounds.

This pain we all feel is an invitation to receive the truth and heal. Your experience of everyday life will show you what requires healing. It is through the mirror of this world that we are able to see our hidden wounds. We can see clearer into our own world by observing what is outside of us. Truth is the master healer, when we spiritually connect and receive the truth; it washes all the pain away leaving joy, peace or bliss.

This pain we all feel is an invitation to receive the truth and heal.

Heart Healing Magic

1) In the last 7 days reflect on an experience that has brought you intense emotional pain. Write it down here.

2) Name the emotion that you felt at the time of this reaction.

3) Look at what this situation may be trying to show you. Allow your ego resistance to guide you to a hidden wound that is asking for healing.

Healing Affirmations

- I see myself in you.

- I am reflected everywhere.

- I bravely see myself in every soul I meet.

- I honour my reflection.

- I own what I see.

Chapter 11 –

Darkness leads

to Light

"Only in the darkness
can you see the stars."

Martin Luther King, Jr.

It's what we judge the most harshly in others that will be the one thing that we need most in our life today. I redeemed my mother from my own judgement by acknowledging the value in her ability to 'block'. I got honest with myself about how arrogant I was to presume that my idea of love: affection, honesty, reciprocity and care, was the most righteous and worthy form of love. Instead my mother showed her love in sacrifice, service, hard work, gifts and academic support. Mum was unable to provide me with the reflection of love that I was yearning for, and instead she modelled for me what would be the most valuable healing tool my life would come to know.

I remember realising that I was finally thin. It had been an epic five year journey that had taught me so much about myself. I had been diligent; I had made the continual and consistent adjustments to manifest a slim body. I remember being so shocked that such a gorgeous figure could have been underneath all that excess weight for so long. It took weeks of seeing myself in shop front windows, getting undressed for the shower and buying new size 10 clothes before I could accept that I was slim. As soon as I recognised this truth, I also recognised that slimming had not been what I had expected it to be.

As soon as I recognised this truth, I also recognised that slimming had not been what I had expected it to be.

I had a long history of lying to myself, and once the excess weight was gone, I realised that I had told myself another lie: That my weight was my only problem! I had been overweight from the age of eight to eighteen. For a decade I believed that life would be better, I would be happier and that I would find love, if only I were slim! Life was better in some ways, but some parts were harder. I was not happier and while I knew men found me attractive, it didn't actually lead me to love!

So, I did the only thing I felt I could: I tried to put all the weight back on again. I started compulsive binge eating in a vain attempt to return to hiding under a comforting shield of blubber, so that I could once again blame my weight for my misery. Yet, I loved my new figure; I was at a major cross-roads. I wasn't able to deny the torrent of emotional pain within, but I had no idea how to get out of it. I reached out to my mum, to talk about the past, about her divorce, about the role I had played in our family. My heart ached to be heard, to be seen and witnessed. I called mum crying, and asked her if we could talk about what happened when I was younger. "Why would you want to do that?" she questioned. For her, the past was over and done with. We were out of all that now, and there was no value in returning to discuss any of it. I pleaded, "Please, I'm not coping, I need to talk about this" A firm and solid "No!" came back through the phone and for the first time I felt I had proof that mum really didn't love me.

As a little girl I had asked repeatedly for cuddles and kisses. Mum had always told me that she just wasn't that type of person. That was hard to accept, I found it easier to believe that she just didn't love me; a convenient lie that would cripple me for years. Who wouldn't spend some time talking to their emotionally volatile daughter? Who couldn't see that she needed to be heard? It was all I needed to know that she really didn't love me. My worst fear had been confirmed. I said that unless we could talk about the past, then I wouldn't be able to have a relationship with her; likewise, Mum said, "I won't talk to you anymore if you keep on insisting about dredging up the past", and then she hung up! At the very moment the phone went dead, lightning like pain shot through my whole body as I crumbled to the floor. My girlfriend, who I shared the house with came running and held me as I howled in pain, writhing with the conclusion that my own mother did in fact - not love me.

I screamed and cried for a while; I couldn't bear the pain I felt, and yet, as moments continued to pass, I became aware of my breath. Air would involuntarily move in, filling my lungs in an inhale, and then find itself back passing out of my body in a subsequent exhale. I was still alive, I was breathing and while I was still in pain, I was still alive.

I had a past that I needed to process, and I respected mum couldn't accompany me on that journey. Somehow hearing her admit that she couldn't talk about the past put all of my other fears into a new perspective. Facing my greatest fear of having my own mother reject me had opened me up to the smallness of my fears. All of a sudden, I didn't care what anyone thought of me, I didn't want to be popular anymore. I realised that I didn't need friends, I didn't need a man.

I abruptly realised that there was nothing left for me to fear and my pain had showed me that I must find healing. It was irrelevant that I had no idea how to heal; I was committed to trying anyway. Healing became my mission, my sole objective, my soul intention, and that alone brought me peace. The singularity of my focus brought great power. My new found clarity allowed me to quickly make important decisions as I asked, will this bring me closer to healing or not? I had survived experiencing my deepest fear; it was time to let my heart rule.

I had survived experiencing my deepest fear;
it was time to let my heart rule.

My awareness of my heart pain was my new light in a dark tunnel because every whim of goodness I felt when contemplating my future was followed reverently. My pain brought me to the clear conclusion that my internal guidance was all I could trust and that my path from now would have to be chosen based on how good I felt about the decisions before me.

Facing the reality of my own mother rejecting me was one of my darkest moments, it felt as though I was falling into a never ending pit of darkness while still sensing the floor beneath me. This moment was so terrifying for my soul, and yet it opened me up to a newfound sense of power. This moment allowed me to find the truth of who I really am: a soul here to heal.

I had found my light, my own internal guidance would lead

me to healing and teach me true love. This wouldn't become clear to me for some time, but it is what you consider your darkness that will inevitably lead you to your light. Thus darkness has value because of what it activates within us as we draw nearer to it. Darkness is our own light suppressed. My mother had a gift for self-protection and self-preservation. She was wise to steer clear of the past because she had accepted that we can't change anything about it. She had a remarkable ability to keep herself safe by blocking anything that might affect her inside. It would be years for me before I could see how I had made mum's closed off stance bad, when in fact it was the healing balm that my soul needed most desperately.

Darkness is our own light suppressed.

Later, when I was learning to develop and protect my gift of empathy I was struggling to spend time in public because of the intensity of emotion that I could feel from everyone around me. A few hours at a shopping centre would send me into an emotional overload, most often ending in bingeing or sleeping to tranquilise me out of overwhelm.

My heart chakra had become so over-active and open from my intent to love others, that it was crippling me. In time I came to see that I had mistakenly judged mum's 'brick-wall'; I had made her ability to 'block' bad and in doing so, I had prevented myself from ever using that aspect for myself. So, while I suffered with emotional overwhelm and paralysing anxiety attacks, it was what I presumed was dark about my mother that would eventually bring me healing.

I felt guided to isolate the trait I had deemed 'dark' within her and looked around at other people who shared this trait. I looked in to see how it showed up in their lives, and I intently searched for the value and benefit I hoped it could bring. Sure enough, those who were able to 'block' were more emotionally secure. They didn't get caught up in other people's dramas. They would only use this attribute if others were starting to encroach on their boundaries. I could see it! I could see the value, the upside, the blessing of this ability to block. I started practicing using it for myself, but it was difficult. As I pushed through my resistance, I noticed that using my ability to block others helped me to feel safer, more secure. I became more capable of defending my boundaries and removing or blocking myself from unwanted emotional turmoil.

It took time for me to remove my judgement from mum; my ego insisted relentlessly that my mum was bad for blocking me out. As I persisted in judging this part of her, I consistently manifested women into my life that would block me, turn away from me, and shut me down. Our patterns are our call to heal, returning time and time again. Mum's ability to disconnect, shut-off and self-protect was something I had made 'bad' because I had assumed that it meant that she didn't love me. The truth was that my mother had always loved me deeply. Releasing my judgement on this attribute of my mother, freed me to step into a new level of power and peace. I finally felt safe to defend and block myself from unwanted energy and influences. The more I practiced blocking, the more I felt I had to give later. I finally felt free to choose when, how and with whom I invested myself.

Heart Healing Magic

1) Contemplate a person within your family who you hold the most judgement against.

2) Name the trait/aspect within this person that you judge them the most harshly for.

3) Write down the blessings, advantages and upsides that you can see other people utilising this same trait/aspect for.

Healing Affirmations

- My shadow teachers lead me to light.

- Darkness leads to light.

- I have seen the darkness; now I see the light.

- Light and dark are one.

- My darkness is my light.

Chapter 12 –
The Gold
in the Dark

"We gain strength, courage, and confidence by each experience in which we really stop to look fear in the face."

Eleanor Roosevelt

Everyone is scared to look into the dark; we think we won't know what we'll find there. It's natural and normal to feel frightened in the presence of darkness but with the aid of a candle what seemed terrifying before can become a magical hunt for treasure. Living a life spent in fear, refusing to look into darkness was a prison I refused to confine myself to. When we begin to see the harrowing events of our past as gifts, we step into a world of receptiveness that allows our healing to unfold beautifully. The brave souls who choose to take up the candle will find treasures beyond measure on their healing journey. As we find the gold in the dark, we emotionally shift into a more empowered state, the emotional pain is released, and we realise how truly loved and protected we really are.

I had dreamed of a magical birth with our first son; calm and serene. My plan for the birth didn't include the use of drugs or intervention, I would allow my son to come forward from the comfort and relaxation of the birthing centre. My vision of the birth involved a white lotus flower gradually opening, unfurling its petals in perfection. I saw myself allowing this process to unfold beautifully and easily. While I had intellectually prepared myself for the birth, I was emotionally unprepared. Giving birth to my son became fertile space for an old wound to surface.

I was about ten hours into labour and my cervix was not dilating. I had been taught in pre-natal classes that the pain had purpose, but according to my understanding these 'sensations' were not doing their job, I was acutely aware that the path before me would only grow in intensity. During the labour I had been hiding my increasing fear from both my midwife and my husband. As the pain and sensations intensified so too did my fear. Could I handle this? I wanted out! After another mind blowing contraction I reached a new conclusion - I wanted a caesarean! Yep, I had swung hard, fast.

The wound that surfaced at this opportune time was a belief that, 'I am powerless to shift out of distress.' In my inner world, once I felt distress it could only end in mutually assured destruction, not exactly a supportive mind-set for giving birth. When I was younger and my parents started fighting, the screaming would always intensify, escalating into outbursts of rage, ending in their separating. These past experiences had conditioned me to think that distress could only escalate.

Nevertheless, everything is always perfect and once my midwife recognised my distress she called the hospital and they began preparing for me to receive an epidural. Everything progressed smoothly and easily once I arrived at the hospital, and holding my little one in my arms melted away all exhaustion and concern.

Fast forward three years and I was preparing to welcome my second child into the world. My first labour experience had taught me a lot about myself and allowed me to turn inward towards my fears and bring healing to my 'distress' wound. I had been preparing for a calm, gentle birth with this second baby, and while I was naive giving birth to my first son, I felt more prepared and experienced to calmly move through whatever unfolded this time.

One day, six weeks before my due date, I was taking my son to his childcare centre for the day. Everything was flowing as normally until I stopped, waiting at an intersection to make a left turn onto a busy main road with one car ahead of me. I saw a break coming in the traffic flow and I assumed that the car in front of me would take it, and I was keen to catch it too. Somehow intently watching the traffic flowing in front of me from my right, I had not seen that the car before me had not in fact gone for the gap. I had just bumped into his rear bumper.

Well I must have bumped into the most irate man in all of Hamilton. I was shocked to see my mistake and got out of the car to see what damage had incurred. As I walked towards the man ahead the obscenities began, "How stupid are you?" "What do you think you're doing?" The verbal abuse only escalated and started becoming more personal and more attacking. I was still in utter shock at my own mistake; this was my very first car accident. I apologised, but this caused no change in him. My pregnant tummy that was looming out before me did little to soften his anger. As his rage began escalating I knew I needed to walk away, move my car and clear my head.

My car had been blocking the traffic behind, and as I walked back to my car I fell apart. I started crying into my hands, overwhelmed by the enormity of this man's response. Luckily for me, a kind angel of a woman had been sitting in her car nearby, closely watching the whole incident unfold. As I was walking back to my car she came rushing to my aid. "Are you okay dear?" she said, "I'm fine, but this guy is blowing everything out of proportion" I responded. She generously asked if I needed help dealing with this guy, and we arranged to both park our cars a little way ahead of the traffic so she could support me. I felt so tenderly watched over and blessed to manifest such a kind helper. I asked her what I needed to do. "Do I just need to give him my contact details and registration?" I asked. "Yes sweetheart" she replied. She coupled her arm in mine and stood by me as I handed my details to the other still very irate driver. Once again, the onslaught of assault began, "This is unnecessary!" my angelic helper declared to the man. Once I gave him my details I turned my back and my new friendly helper and I walked back to our cars. Once I was home, I called on a dear friend. "Okay, listen to what I've manifested this morning" I said, "Can you help me to see the message in this?" Sure enough we paid close attention to how the event felt for me, we focused in on what emotional states this experience had evoked in me.

My girlfriend had identified that I felt distressed by the car accident and meeting this highly irate man had caused it to escalate. Straight away, we remembered the role that 'distress' had played in my previous labour experience and I remembered how all of my prayers and thoughts were focused on creating a calm and smooth birthing experience for me and my soon to be born little girl. Here was my blessing, I'd manifested an experience where emotional distress would be the outcome. Circumstances were forged so that I would be tempted to play out the escalating distress that was so familiar to me and remind myself once again how powerless I felt in the presence of my own distress. And yet, in circumstances that could have perfectly allowed me to play out the belief that 'I am powerless to shift out of distress' I chose to walk away - Boom! This irate argumentative, attacking man gave me every reason to buy into the drama, react and allow myself to let my distress escalate; but I had witnessed myself choosing something new.

I knew this experience had come to show me that I had healed. It was a tremendous gift for me to experience this confirmation of my healing, just weeks prior to giving birth again. In my world, everything is a blessing, and manifesting this irate man into my world was no exception. He was a powerful shadow teacher, helping me to reclaim my power under distress. I saw the whole exchange as a divinely orchestrated healing experience preparing me perfectly for the birth of my second child. Sure enough, some six weeks later I truly felt prepared for a beautiful birth experience. I remained calm, and focused on allowing. I stayed connected to my feelings, communicated honestly with my support team. I was blessed to manifest a smooth and safe three hour labour; it was my miracle.

He was a powerful shadow teacher, helping me to reclaim my power under distress.

As you find the upside and blessings of what you thought were bad experiences, you open to embrace duality and feel an emotional release. There are always gifts to be found within our painful experiences. When we explore, question and allow ourselves to open up to the gifts that we've received, they will become clear. Understanding our pain from a new perspective brings relief, you can rejoice knowing how it has served you in ways you never realised before. From this new view-point you can begin to see that there is value and purpose to everything that you have been through. Claim the gifts and you reclaim your power.

There are always gifts to be found within our painful experiences.

Heart Healing Magic

1)   Look at one of your darkest experiences. What were the gifts of this experience? What was the upside, and how has this experience benefitted you?

2)   Name the one trait within yourself that you judge as being 'bad' or 'dark'. Write down what the benefits of this trait are?

3)   Think of a person from your past that has showed up as very dark. Identify the one trait that you feel was darkest in them. Now, write down the benefits and value inherent in that trait.

Healing Affirmations

- Into darkness, I seek the gold.

- Resistance guides me forward.

- I now seek out all of me.

- What I need is lying in the dark.

- Freedom lies in darkness.

Chapter 13 –
Our Pain
is our Purpose

"I want to honour my soul today.
May that always be my first love,
my first choice.

I feel I am finally understanding
why I am here.

I am here so that I might love.
So that I might love my heart, my
mind, my soul and my body."

S. C. Lourie

I now see that we are all on our own healing journey. Our pain is our own personal invitation to the healing journey, and we are all broken open more than we can bear in order to invite us to develop our greatness within; our personal gold. It is this treasure that will ultimately bring us to our peace, power and purpose.

Being raised in a home where heart wounds ruled, where emotional turmoil was a constant and where I was powerless to create any change, would become the breeding ground for my soul's purpose. I was broken open time and time again, overwhelmed by the pain I saw around me. The difficulty these circumstances created for me became my opportunity to cultivate the skills required for my purpose.

Feeling so desperately unloved by my own family, motivated me to extend myself towards anyone in need of love. I felt compelled to offer others the listening ear, acceptance, consideration or quality time. I keenly observed their response and learnt a great deal about love. In seeking to offer what I didn't comprehend I found my own original, pure concept and practice of love, which has become a deep treasure in my life. While I was fueled by the fear of my own 'un-lovability', I chose to stretch myself, unfurling into an understanding of love that I couldn't find. I realised that there can be no failure when offering love, just varied results. When I hold the intention of love, love finds a way to come through me.

I knew how to offer love to others, but I had had no practice giving it to myself. I knew how to listen to others, but had never really heard myself. I could naturally offer acceptance to anyone, but I had no idea how to offer this gift to myself. It was ironic that I felt I had so much love to give others, yet I felt empty and incapable of offering myself anything remotely kind or loving. I had made the assumption that if I could make enough people happy, then I would eventually find myself happy! Well, that had not been true for me. My shallow attempt to love other's came from my fear that if I didn't give love to others then no one would love me in return. I was trapped in giving everything I had to others, in a vain attempt to receive for myself. Pain became my great ally; I paid attention to how much I ached giving so profusely to others, I would do anything to be out of that pain, even if it meant learning to love myself!

I was trapped in giving everything I had to others, in a vain attempt to receive for myself.

Breaking open and breaking down at age 23, leaving my job and leaving everything I had known to head to Cairns was the catalyst that would alter my entire world and allow me to align with my soul's purpose. My ego had concocted an insidious plan for my safe-keeping – which was that I found myself locked in repeating patterns that were intended to keep me 'safe'. The familiarity of the repeating pain had triggered an opening in my heart and an opening in my awareness, which became my doorway to freedom. My repeating pattern showed me that the genesis of my wounds was within. I was guided to use my own emotional pain to track down the lies I had unconsciously concluded that were beneath all of the mess that had filled my love life.

During my escape to Cairns, I switched off from everyone else. Just one year prior I had been trapped in a popularity game where I would invest myself heavily in superficial friendships; we all knew each other's names but we never confided our truth in one another. I gave to everyone in an attempt to lift myself up. I would extend myself so far, that when I was alone I would feel drained, deflated and empty. I was left bitter that the love, help and support I gave generously to all of my 'friends' never found its way back to me. Once in Cairns, I gave myself permission to ignore everyone else but myself. If giving all of myself to others had been destructive for me, surely there could be value in investing now in me.

Every day would be a feast of asking myself, "What would you like to do Lysy?" I would wear the clothes I loved, irrespective of what people thought. I would take myself out for a yummy lunch or to a movie. I made myself my own priority for the first time in my life. I would work selling dresses by day, and fall into myself by journal at night. I was intent on hearing, feeling, and knowing all of the most private details of my heart; actually learning how to confide in myself. I was scared I was selfish, but I didn't care; I felt free to do whatever I wanted for the very first time in my life.

I realised that I believed that I couldn't help myself, and that was so abhorrent to my soul that I did everything I could to help others in an attempt to mask my own powerlessness. I would stretch myself to try and help other people feel better, because I had given up on ever feeling better myself. A deep hopelessness and depression lay beneath my need to give to others; and it was caused by a powerful collection of beliefs that remained unhealed as wounds in my heart. My vain attempt to fix the problems of other's was my attempt to distract myself from my own pain.

In Cairns I acknowledged the depth of my sensitivity and I learnt to embrace my tenderness and vulnerability. I also discovered how deeply empathic I was and came to respect why the pain in others had caused such real physical pain within my own body. For a time, I withdrew from public places, I would shy away from contact with anyone, seeking first to understand and heal my own heart first. I knew there were times when I did go out in to public places when I felt infected, overwhelmed by the immensity of what I felt in other's. I realised that I was powerless to effect change in their souls, but what if their pain was a mirror to my own? I began using the feelings I could sense in others to bring awareness to my own heart wounds. If someone who walked past me was feeling bitter, I would find the place within myself where bitterness hid. Through this process I discovered the power of being with my feelings, as I stayed with them, received their messages and lovingly heard all they had to share I began a process of emotionally digesting a lifetime of hurt that needed to be heard. The more I stayed with myself, offering acceptance to what I found within, the more trust and love I developed for myself.

I realised that I was powerless to effect change in their souls, but what if their pain was a mirror to my own?

While I sought healing through other professionals, their skill set and care did little to release my pain. My healing would be prolonged, it would occur over the progression of a number of years while I dipped my toes in every known strategy and theory of healing I could find. By trial and error I experimented, trying new concepts out on myself. After years of gleaning some of the best strategies I could find I decided it was time to stop reading and start tapping into my own intuition and heavenly guidance to aid my journey.

As I stopped seeking answers outside of myself, my progress increased rapidly, as did my results. My heart's desires would continually manifest as I deepened into my healing journey. Personal answers to my prayers would clarify the subtle details that would lead to new breakthroughs and epiphanies. I did not attempt to heal my client's; I sought to connect them to their own guidance and taught the principles of healing so that they could experience self healing just as I had.

Healing is a rich journey where daily messages, miraculous manifestations and continual guidance are available to us all. I feel fulfilled as I lead people back to a deep connection with themselves, their own feelings, and their own sense of trust in their higher power to support them in their self healing process. In all of my experience I have learnt that:

- Everything is for our highest good.

- We are always exactly where we need to be.

- Heavenly guidance, answers and protection are always available to us.

- Healing can be fun; a magical journey opening us to the unknown so that we can receive everything that we desire in the process.

- We always manifest friends and messengers into our lives in order to support our path.

- Everything is two-sided and when we experience great pain around one experience, it certainly will hold the potential for a composite gift of equal or greater value.

- When we embrace the moments that have hurt us the most we open up to finding our purpose.

- With thanks to our shadow teachers, it is those who have shown us the most darkness who actually lead us into the light.

- What hurts us the most in this life will miraculously become our purpose, passion and ultimately bring us peace.

Healing is a rich journey where daily messages, miraculous manifestations and continual guidance are available to us all.

Heart Healing Magic

1)   Recall an event that caused you suffering. Ask your higher power to guide you as you consider how this event has become a blessing in your life.

2)   Reflect over what you feel has been your most painful experience in life to date. What skills, gifts or attributes did that event cause to flourish within you?

3)   What has been the purpose you have found from the pain you have experienced?

Healing Affirmations

- My pain calls me to my greatness.

- My pain prepares me to serve.

- The things that hurt me prepare me.

- My hurt cultivates my power.

- Within my wounds, lies my power.

About The Author

Lysa Black is a Heart Healer. Dedicating 10 years to healing her own heart opened Lysa to her natural gift of healing presence. Being intuitively guided to heal her own anxiety, binge eating and pattern of break-ups led Lysa to her soul purpose. She is a highly sensitive empath who has the superpower of 'reading' hearts; Lysa can relay information about your current and past emotional experiences, life theme's and patterns as well as spiritual gifts and soul purpose. Author of *Heart Healing* and *Divine Purpose,* Lysa's open heart, self-acceptance and compassionate presence creates an atmosphere where others can access their own inner healer. She has professionally stood besides thousands of clients over a span of 8 years; she is an internationally sought after guide and mentor for those seeking to authentically align in purpose as Healers and Leaders. Lysa lives with her husband and two young children in Northland, New Zealand.

See Lysa:

Facebook: https://www.facebook.com/EmpressLysaBlack/

Instagram: https://www.instagram.com/empresslysablack/

YouTube: https://www.youtube.com/c/LysaBlack

Website: http://www.lysablack.com/

www.ingramcontent.com/pod-product-compliance
Lightning Source LLC
Chambersburg PA
CBHW071435090426
42737CB00011B/1664